WRITTEN BY SETH
GRAHAME-SMITH

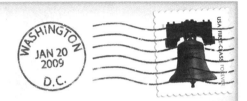

PARDON MY PRESIDENT
READY-TO-MAIL APOLOGIES
FOR 8 YEARS OF GEORGE W. BUSH

★ ★ ★ ★ ★ ★   JUST TEAR AND SEND!   ★ ★ ★ ★ ★ ★

QUIRK BOOKS
PHILADELPHIA

For T. Gordon Smith
A true Texan

Copyright © 2008 by Seth Grahame-Smith

All rights reserved. No part of this book may be reproduced in any form without written permission from the publisher.

Library of Congress Cataloging in Publication Number: 2008923773

ISBN: 978-1-59474-287-3

Printed in Malaysia
Typeset in Adobe Garamond and Apollo MT

Designed by Karen Onorato
Logo illustrated by Jude Buffum

Distributed in North America by Chronicle Books
680 Second Street
San Francisco, CA 94107

10 9 8 7 6 5 4 3 2 1

Quirk Books
215 Church Street
Philadelphia, PA 19106
www.quirkbooks.com

"I think we agree, the past is over."
—*George W. Bush, Pittsburgh, Pennsylvania (May 2000)*

Dear Reader,

When rational people make a mistake, they apologize. It's the quickest way to settle an issue and get on with life. It demonstrates strength and character.

George W. Bush made an awful lot of mistakes during his presidency.

We're still waiting for an apology.

Just look at us. The economy's in flames. Energy and healthcare costs have reached sickening levels. We're spending like a monkey with a stolen wallet. The ice caps are melting (probably from the heat thrown off by the economy). Congress has more corruption than a John Grisham novel. The Taliban and Al Qaeda are mounting a comeback tour (strangely, with Toby Keith opening). America is the most despised nation on earth, and all we can do is scream at one another about who loves Jesus more.

I'm sick of it, and I don't think I'm alone.

The thing is, I love America. And not just in that "magnetic yellow ribbon on my SUV" way. I mean, *really* love it. I love America so much that it saddens me to see its greatness diminished by a fear-mongering, bumbling, pandering, partisan, elitist, disengaged, disingenuous, and unduly arrogant chief executive.

These letters are a tiny attempt to reclaim some of that greatness by doing something President Bush seems unwilling to do—apologize to the dozens of individuals, groups, nations, inanimate objects, animals, and concepts that he and his fellow ideologues have screwed over during their eight-year occupation of the Oval Office.

These letters are also an attempt to make you laugh, cringe, and give the U.S. Postal Service a much-needed shot in the arm.

So if you find one that tickles your funny (or angry) bone, sign it, stamp it, and let somebody know how you feel.

And remember . . . sometimes love means having to say you're sorry.

Seth Grahame-Smith

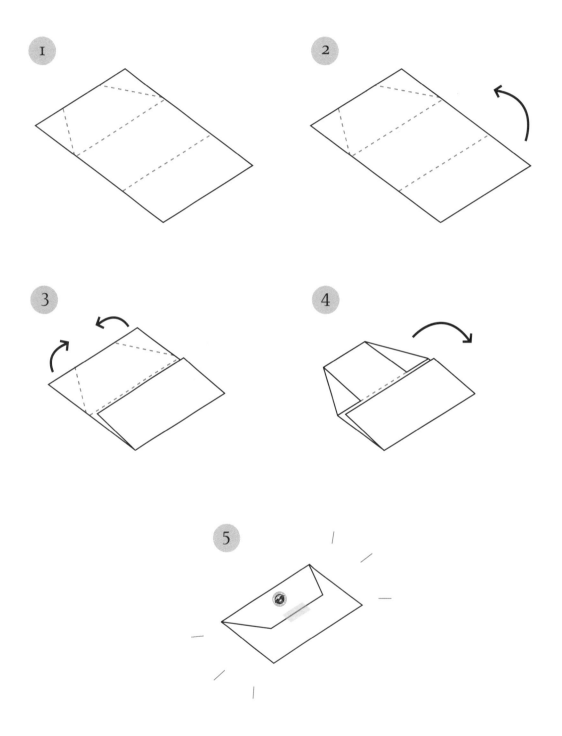

THE RESIDENTS OF CRAWFORD, TEXAS
c/o The Honorable David Posten, Mayor
6719 N. Lone Star Pkwy.
Crawford, TX 76638

Dear Residents of Crawford,

Howdy! Life certainly was simpler before the Bushes blew into town, wasn't it? When CNN asked one local to describe Crawford back in August of 2001, he said, "It's hot, it's dry and full of snakes." Those were the days.

Having the "Western White House" in your backyard has been quite a boon to some of y'all. You've fed hungry hordes of reporters, sold commemorative mugs bearing Crawford's favorite son (who moved there in 1999), and become a symbol of the Bush presidency. Which brings me to the apology . . .

You've become a symbol of the Bush presidency.

By the summer of 2007, Dubya had whiled away (all or part of) 418 days on his Crawford ranch (that's 15 percent of his presidency spent on vacation, making him our most relaxed Commander in Chief ever).

What's that? Don't think one person can determine the image of a whole town? C'mon, you're only eighteen miles from Waco. Don't think a politician can leave an indelible stain on a quiet little hamlet? Why don't you ask the folks in Chappaquiddick if the jokes have gotten old yet.

But there's good news. The spotlight will begin to fade the moment he leaves office. Who knows? Maybe he'll even pack up and head back to his native Connecticut. And if he does, what will Crawford look like without the Bushes? My guess is, a lot like it did before they arrived. It'll still be hot. It'll still be dry.

But at least the snakes will be gone.

Oh snap,

THE RESIDENTS OF CRAWFORD, TEXAS
C/O THE HONORABLE DAVID POSTEN, MAYOR
6719 N. LONE STAR PKWY.
CRAWFORD, TX 76638

TARGET
Attn: Mr. Robert J. Ulrich, CEO
1000 Nicollet Mall
Minneapolis, MN 55403

Dear Mr. Ulrich,

On behalf of the Bush administration, I'd like to apologize for the actions of Mr. Claude A. Allen, the president's former top advisor on domestic policy. Despite the fact that he earned $160,000 a year, Mr. Allen apparently felt the need to steal from Target. According to legal documents, he made six fraudulent returns totaling more than $1,000 between October 2005 and January 2006, before finally being brought to justice at your Gaithersburg, Maryland, store.

During a court appearance, Mr. Allen tearfully blamed his behavior on the stress he'd felt as the head of the White House's response to Hurricane Katrina. What stress, Mr. Allen? The White House had no response to Katrina, remember?

As you know, Mr. Allen was ordered to pay $850 in restitution to your company—less than he reportedly stole. I just pray that the $150 difference doesn't put too much strain on Target's bottom line.

Blessings,

U.S. DEPARTMENT OF HOMELAND APOLOGY

TARGET
ATTN: MR. ROBERT J. ULRICH, CEO
1000 NICOLLET MALL
MINNEAPOLIS, MN 55403

TEACHERS

c/o National Education Association
1201 16th St. NW
Washington, DC 20036-3290

Dear Teachers,

First of all, thank you. You don't hear it enough, and that's a shame. The very fact that I'm able to write this letter is a testament to the good work performed by educators across the United States of America. But I worry about how much longer you'll be able to do that good work (and yes, I began the sentence with a conjunction).

Not because your salaries aren't keeping up with inflation, or because the man who said "I want to be the education president" vetoed a paltry 5 percent increase in education spending in 2007. And not because the president's "No Child Left Behind" program was so drastically underfunded and unfair that it became known as "No Child Left."

No, I'm worried because President Bush's secretary of education, Rod Paige, called the National Education Association a "terrorist organization."

I'm sorry, teachers, but it appears that you've been added to the Axis of Evil. Given the president's record on foreign policy, it probably won't be long before we begin bombing you.

Studiously,

U.S. DEPARTMENT OF HOMELAND APOLOGY

2001 · MISTAKES WERE MADE · 2009

TEACHERS

C/O NATIONAL EDUCATION ASSOCIATION

1201 16TH ST. NW

WASHINGTON, DC 20036-3290

MR. ALBERTO GONZALES
c/o Greater Talent Network
437 Fifth Ave.
New York, NY 10016

Dear Mr. Gonzales,

As attorney general, you appeared before the Senate Judiciary Committee on April 19, 2007, to answer questions about your role in the (possibly improper) firings of seven U.S. attorneys.

During that hearing, you answered the senators' questions with some form of "I don't recall," "I have no recollection," or "I don't remember" a total of sixty-four times.

Mr. Gonzales, I apologize for your rotten luck.

Though rare, early-onset Alzheimer's can affect patients as young as age forty or fifty. You were only fifty-one years old at the time of your testimony, but clearly the disease had already taken hold.

Please know that you're in my thoughts and prayers as you continue to fight along with the five million Americans affected by this terrible illness. A donation has been made in your name to the Alzheimer's Association in Chicago.

Mr. Gonzales, "I don't recall" a braver government official.

Sincerely,

U.S. DEPARTMENT OF HOMELAND APOLOGY

WE'RE MADE MISTAKES · 2001 2009

MR. ALBERTO GONZALES
C/O GREATER TALENT NETWORK
437 FIFTH AVE.
NEW YORK, NY 10016

PEOPLE OF FRANCE
c/o Assemblée Nationale
126, rue de l'Université
F-75355 Paris 07 SP
France

Dear People of France,

In March 2003, a Republican congressmen from Ohio, Bob Ney, ordered that all French fries sold in the U.S. Capitol be renamed "freedom fries," in retaliation for France's opposition to invading Iraq.

In a statement, Ney said:

> "This action today is a small, but symbolic, effort to show the strong displeasure many on Capitol Hill have with our so-called ally, France."

I apologize. You see, Mr. Ney is an idiot.

If it's any consolation, a few years later he was sent to federal prison for corruption.

Sincèrement,

P.S.: Thanks again for helping us win the Revolutionary War.

U.S. DEPARTMENT OF HOMELAND APOLOGY

PEOPLE OF FRANCE
C/O ASSEMBLÉE NATIONALE
126, RUE DE L'UNIVERSITÉ
F-75355 PARIS 07 SP
FRANCE

HER MAJESTY QUEEN ELIZABETH II
Buckingham Palace
London SW1A 1AA
United Kingdom

Your Majesty,

On 7 May 2007, you stood beside President George W. Bush on the White House south lawn for a welcoming ceremony in honor of Your Majesty's state visit. During his remarks, the president misspoke, suggesting that Your Majesty had visited America in 1776. The rather foolish gaffe was met with laughter from guests and reporters alike.

Pausing for the laughter, Mr. Bush turned to Your Majesty and winked, apparently ignorant of (or with stunning disregard for) the inappropriateness of such a gesture. Your Majesty returned the wink with a disapproving glare, which the president mocked as "a look that only a mother could give a child."

I beg to differ with Mr. Bush. If I may, I believe that Your Majesty gave him a look that only a distinguished head of state could give a brash, overconfident cowboy with no regard for protocol or diplomacy.

Please accept my deepest apologies for his behavior.

Humbly,

U.S. DEPARTMENT OF HOMELAND APOLOGY
MISTAKES WERE MADE
2001 2009

HER MAJESTY QUEEN ELIZABETH II
BUCKINGHAM PALACE
LONDON SW1A 1AA
UNITED KINGDOM

HER EXCELLENCY ANGELA MERKEL
Chancellor
Bundeskanzleramt
Willy Brand Straße 1
10178 Berlin
Germany

Dear Chancellor Merkel,

At the 2006 G-8 summit in St. Petersburg, Russia, President Bush approached you from behind and began rubbing your shoulders. You immediately grimaced and shrugged him off, but it was too late. The whole embarrassing affair was captured by cameras and shown countless times around the world.

I ask that you forgive the president for his actions. It's not that he meant to belittle you or somehow suggest that you shouldn't be afforded the same level of respect as other heads of state just because you're a woman. Quite the contrary. In his mind, he was simply offering a gesture of genuine affection.

The truth is, Madame Chancellor, Mr. Bush simply doesn't have the capacity to distinguish between appropriate and inappropriate behavior. I apologize for any discomfort his actions may have caused you.

Respectfully,

U.S. DEPARTMENT OF HOMELAND APOLOGY
2001 · 2009
MISTAKES WERE MADE

AFFIX
POSTAGE
HERE

HER EXCELLENCY ANGELA MERKEL
CHANCELLOR
BUNDESKANZLERAMT
WILLY BRAND STRAßE 1
10178 BERLIN
GERMANY

PRESIDENT JAMES BUCHANAN
c/o The James Buchanan Foundation
1120 Marietta Ave.
Lancaster, PA 17603

Dear President Buchanan,

For more than a century now, historians have repeatedly placed you at the top of their "worst presidents of all time" lists. And with good reason.

You were terrible.

From 1857 to 1861, you sat idly by while the Union tore itself apart. You pissed and moaned about the illegality of Southern secession but claimed that the federal government was powerless to stop it. Even if you hadn't sympathized with slave owners (and you did), you lacked the very backbone necessary to stem the tide of Southern rebellion. By the time you left office, seven states had broken away to form the Confederacy, taking most of their forts and arsenals with them. The stage was set for the Civil War, a horrific conflict that lasted more than four years and claimed over 600,000 lives.

Nice going, asshole.

Still, you're owed an apology, for though you were truly awful, we now know that you were, at best, the second-worst U.S. president of all time.

Funny, isn't it? That ultimately, it was your hesitation to go to war that secured your place in the colostomy bag of history. And that it took a Republican—a *Republican* of all things—to come in and clean up the mess you'd left behind.

Here's hoping history has a sense of irony.

Decisively yours,

U.S. DEPARTMENT OF HOMELAND APOLOGY
MISTAKES... WERE MADE
2001 2009

PRESIDENT JAMES BUCHANAN
C/O THE JAMES BUCHANAN FOUNDATION
1120 MARIETTA AVE.
LANCASTER, PA 17603

BIG OIL
c/o Exxon Mobil
5959 Las Colinas Blvd.
Irving, TX 75039-2298

Dear Big Oil,

I am so, so sorry.

President Bush just didn't do enough.

Yes, he surrounded himself with your friends, like Condoleezza Rice, who served on the board of Chevron (and had a tanker named after her), and Dick Cheney, who ran an energy company before taking office. Yes, the president was an ex–oil man. Yes, he invited oil companies to the White House to create energy policy.

But to what end?

When Mr. Bush took office, oil was hovering at a dismal $25 a barrel. By 2008, that price had only quadrupled. Good, but not good enough. Why not $600 or $800 a barrel? And why were only six of the world's ten biggest corporations yours? Why not all ten? How are companies like Exxon Mobil supposed to scrape by on $40 billion in profit in a single year?

I have this recurring dream: President Bush is walking out of the White House on the last day of his term. Slowly, tearfully, he makes his way to a waiting limousine, just like Liam Neeson at the end of *Schindler's List*. He pauses every few feet and looks in the eyes of the oil executives who've gathered to see him off. The president clutches one of their lapels and begins to sob again, saying the same thing over and over . . .

"I could've made you one more dollar."

Indeed, he could have.

Crudely,

U.S. DEPARTMENT OF HOMELAND APOLOGY
MISTAKES WERE MADE
2001 · 2009

BIG OIL
C/O EXXON MOBIL
5959 LAS COLINAS BLVD.
IRVING, TX 75039-2298

MR. SIEGFRIED ENGELMANN AND MS. ELAINE C. BRUNER
c/o SRA/McGraw-Hill
220 East Danieldale Rd.
Desoto, TX 75115-2490

Dear Mr. Engelmann and Ms. Bruner,

On September 11, 2001, President George W. Bush was reading your story called "The Pet Goat" to a group of elementary school students when he learned that America was under attack. Famously, he continued to sit there—clutching your book—for seven minutes. Since then the incident has been widely scrutinized, most notably in the film *Fahrenheit 9/11*. It's been lampooned on *The Daily Show* and parodied in music videos.

But amid the hype, everyone forgot about your story.

First, the title of the work is "The Pet Goat" not "My Pet Goat," as many have mistakenly titled it. Second, "The Pet Goat" isn't the name of a book; rather it is one story in your collection *Reading Mastery: Level 2, Storybook 1 (Reading Mastery: Rainbow Edition)*. Third, few people even know what the story is about.

It begins with the powerfully simple "A girl got a pet goat." With these six words, you establish not only the two main characters, but their relationship as well. "She played with her goat in her yard." I can almost smell the crisp, chimney-kissed autumn air as girl and beast frolic in piles of freshly fallen leaves. "The goat did some things that made the girl's dad mad." Ah, conflict! Faced with expulsion, the goat struggles to endear himself to the girl's father (my only criticism is that the parallels between the goat and Shakespeare's titular Coriolanus become a tad deafening in this part). Whether he achieves redemption or not, I'll leave that to the reader to discover.

Writers deserve to have their work judged on its merits. Your story has been denied its due respect. For that, I—along with the entire literary community—offer an apology.

All my best,

U.S. DEPARTMENT OF HOMELAND APOLOGY

MR. SIEGFRIED ENGELMANN AND
MS. ELAINE C. BRUNER
C/O SRA/MCGRAW-HILL
220 EAST DANIELDALE RD.
DESOTO, TX 75115-2490

MR. ALAN COLMES
Fox News Channel
1211 Avenue of the Americas, 18th Floor
New York, NY 10036

Dear Mr. Colmes,

I'm writing to inform you that you may have cause for legal action against Mr. Sean Hannity, your cohost on the Fox News program "Hannity & Colmes."

It is the finding of a panel of independent experts that Mr. Hannity has repeatedly and knowingly subjected you to sexual harassment, as outlined in Title VII of the Civil Rights Act of 1964.

He has done so by forcing you to watch him fellate George W. Bush for eight years.

I deeply regret any pain and suffering this reprehensible behavior has caused, and I strongly encourage you to seek compensatory and punitive damages.

Sincerely,

U.S. DEPARTMENT OF
HOMELAND APOLOGY
2001 · 2009
MISTAKES WERE MADE

MR. ALAN COLMES
FOX NEWS CHANNEL
1211 AVENUE OF THE AMERICAS, 18TH FLOOR
NEW YORK, NY 10036

AFFIX
POSTAGE
HERE

MR. ADAM CLYMER
c/o The New York Times
620 Eighth Ave.
New York, NY 10018

Dear Mr. Clymer,

On September 4, 2000, George W. Bush called you a "major-league asshole" while on stage at a campaign rally in Naperville, Illinois (probably because you had written several pieces for the *New York Times* that were less than flattering to his candidacy). You may recall that it caused quite a sensation. You may also recall that Mr. Bush never apologized for his comment.

Mr. Clymer, I have conducted an investigation into this matter and determined that you are not, in fact, an asshole—let alone one of major-league proportions. Here are a few facts I uncovered:

Until your retirement in 2003 (no doubt expedited by the stress of being branded an "asshole" by the leader of the free world) you were a highly respected journalist and biographer with four decades of experience—three of them spent covering American politics for the *Times*.

You received the prestigious Carey McWilliams Award from the American Political Science Association. Prior recipients include Jim Lehrer, Molly Ivins, and William Kristol.

In 1985, your only child, Jane Emily, was killed by a drunk driver. You and your wife of more than forty years, Ann, established a memorial scholarship in her name at the University of Vermont, where your daughter had been a student. To this day, you make a point of getting to know each and every recipient of that scholarship.

Clearly, sir, Mr. Bush was mistaken in his assessment of your character. And since he has thus refused to apologize, I consider it my duty to do so on his behalf.

Very truly yours,

MR. ADAM CLYMER
C/O THE NEW YORK TIMES
620 EIGHTH AVE.
NEW YORK, NY 10018

THE COLOR ORANGE
c/o The National Gallery of Art
600 Constitution Ave. NW
Washington, DC 20565

Dear Orange,

Once upon a time, you were the color of deliciousness and joy.

Now you're the color of imminent terror.

Sorry.

Sincerely,

U.S. DEPARTMENT OF HOMELAND APOLOGY

THE COLOR ORANGE
C/O THE NATIONAL GALLERY OF ART
600 CONSTITUTION AVE. NW
WASHINGTON, DC 20565

THE UNITED STATES ARMED FORCES

c/o Office of the Chairman of the Joint Chiefs of Staff
Attn: Chairman's Public Correspondence Branch/SJS
400 Joint Staff Pentagon
Washington, DC 20318-0400

Dear Soldiers,

Thank you.

You're the baddest, bravest, most professional fighting force in the history of the world, and I sleep better knowing you're there. I appreciate your service and sacrifice, and the freedoms they protect. However, I'm appalled by the way you've been treated by some of our leaders here at home.

When you were ordered to topple Saddam Hussein, you carried out your mission with breakneck speed and remarkable efficiency. But since then, as you've fought to keep the peace in a critically unstable country, you've been consistently short-changed by your government and your Commander in Chief.

You've seen your deployments extended from twelve to fifteen months. You've had to rely on private donations to buy reliable body armor. You've taken to welding scrap metal onto Humvees to provide protection against IEDs. Your combat pay is a measly $225 a month, which the Pentagon considered cutting to $150 before the public heard about it. Your wounded have been housed in disgraceful, mold-ridden facilities. You've been stretched to the breaking point, and you've endured it with quiet toughness, as always.

Washington owes each one of you an apology. Politicians are fond of the old saying "freedom isn't free." They're right.

And neither are the men and women who protect it for us.

With gratitude,

U.S. DEPARTMENT OF HOMELAND APOLOGY
MISTAKES WERE MADE
2001 · 2009

THE UNITED STATES ARMED FORCES
C/O OFFICE OF THE CHAIRMAN OF THE JOINT CHIEFS OF STAFF
ATTN: CHAIRMAN'S PUBLIC CORRESPONDENCE BRANCH/SJS
400 JOINT STAFF PENTAGON
WASHINGTON, DC 20318-0400

RUSH LIMBAUGH
The Rush Limbaugh Show
2 Penn Plaza, 17th Floor
New York, NY 10121

Dear Rush,

I'd like to apologize on behalf of President Bush—not for Iraq, or Katrina, or any of the other so-called issues that we're all sick of the liberal media making such a big fuss over, but for the Medicare Prescription Drug Benefit, which took effect in 2006. No, not because it'll cost taxpayers up to $1.2 trillion—three times what the administration promised—but because it prevents Medicare from negotiating discounts with drug manufacturers (as the Department of Veterans Affairs is able to do).

That means that when you become eligible for Medicare in 2016, you'll be paying higher prices for your prescriptions than is necessary. (If you were a veteran, you'd be able to get those same drugs for less money, but during Vietnam you were declared 4-F for having a cyst on your ass.)

As a recovering drug addict, I know this issue is near and dear to your heart. After all, what if you relapse and start popping OxyContin-like breath mints again? Thanks to the Bush administration, you'd be paying out your cyst-ridden ass for them.

And that, sir, is not the way things ought to be.

With excellence,

U.S. DEPARTMENT OF HOMELAND APOLOGY
"MISTAKES WERE MADE"
2001   2009

_____

_____

_____

RUSH LIMBAUGH
THE RUSH LIMBAUGH SHOW
2 PENN PLAZA, 17TH FLOOR
NEW YORK, NY 10121

MR. RICHARD CLARKE
Good Harbor Consulting, LLC
2101 Wilson Blvd., Suite 100
Arlington, VA 22201

Dear Mr. Clarke,

Hey there! Remember when you were special advisor to the president, and you warned Condoleezza Rice that we should be paying more attention to Al Qaeda? Remember that memo you sent to her on January 25, 2001? You know, the one that said:

> "Al Qida [sic] is not some narrow, little terrorist issue that needs to be included in broader regional policy . . . we would make a major error if we underestimated the challenge [it] poses."

Remember that? How you called it an "active, organized, major force"? How you recommended funding the Northern Alliance in their fight against the Taliban or your suggestion about issuing warnings against giving safe haven to Al Qaeda in Afghanistan?

Oh, and remember how you asked for a principals-level meeting on the matter and included two preexisting strategies for dealing with Al Qaeda?

Yeah . . . I'm sorry nobody listened.

Kind regards,

U.S. DEPARTMENT OF HOMELAND APOLOGY

MR. RICHARD CLARKE
GOOD HARBOR CONSULTING, LLC
2101 WILSON BLVD., SUITE 100
ARLINGTON, VA 22201

AFFIX
POSTAGE
HERE

SEN. MAX CLELAND
c/o Sen. Saxby Chambliss
416 Russell Senate Office Bldg.
Washington, DC 20510

Dear Senator Cleland,

In the 2002 senate race, your opponent, Saxby Chambliss (who never served in the military) said that you (a decorated war veteran who lost three limbs in Vietnam) "lacked the courage to lead." He even ran a commercial featuring you, Osama Bin Laden, and Saddam Hussein. It's been widely speculated that, in private, Karl Rove helped cook up this line of attack during the race. A race that you lost. And it's for that loss, and the indignity it brought to you, that I am deeply, sincerely sorry.

Senator, I know how angry the memories of that campaign must make you feel. But if you let them get under your skin, they've won. We cannot, we shall not, resort to their level of cheap smears and petty name calling.

I mean, can you imagine how counterproductive it would be if I called Saxby Chambliss a gutless puddle of cat vomit? A miserable chickenshit who weaseled out of Vietnam (where you were busy getting your limbs blown off) because he had "bad knees"? Or if I insinuated that he got those "bad knees" from fellating teenage boys in the same dark alley where he ran a coat-hanger abortion clinic?

No. Of course you can't, because those insinuations would be childish and, at least partially, untrue. As would suggesting that I pray for Jesus to rip off Saxby's arms and legs and give them to you, or that the name "Saxby Chambliss" sounds like a $3 perfume for French transsexuals.

I wouldn't dream of saying such things, because I'm better than that, Senator. We're better than that. Thank you for your service to our country.

Respectfully,

U.S. DEPARTMENT OF HOMELAND APOLOGY

MISTAKES WERE MADE

2001 2009

SEN. MAX CLELAND
C/O SEN. SAXBY CHAMBLISS
416 RUSSELL SENATE OFFICE BLDG.
WASHINGTON, DC 20510

THE PEOPLE OF DARFUR

c/o President Omar Hassan al-Bashir
People's Palace
PO Box 281
Khartoum, Sudan

Dear People of Darfur,

Since 2003, hundreds of thousands of you have been slaughtered in the ongoing clash between Sudan-backed troops and rebel militias. Innocent men have been executed, women gang raped, babies dismembered, and entire villages destroyed. Starvation and disease run rampant among the more than two million of your compatriots who have been displaced.

The problem has been exacerbated by your "president," a miserable prick named Omar Hassan al-Bashir. He's jailed and executed witnesses who've spoken out about the atrocities committed by his soldiers. He's covered up evidence of mass graves. He's even prevented international aid from being delivered to you. He's also defied the international community by refusing to allow UN peacekeepers into the region.

I bet you're wondering, "Why doesn't somebody make him?" I mean, no offense, but it would take a Buick full of Navy SEALs about ten minutes and three bullets to bring the Sudanese army to its knees—and even less time for the CIA to sprinkle heart-attack powder in Omar's corn flakes. So where's the cavalry? Didn't President Bush admit that your plight was genocide? Didn't he pledge that "the United States will not avert our eyes from a crisis that challenges the conscience of the world"?

Um . . . well . . . see, the thing is, we're sort of bogged down in a more profitable part of the world at the moment.

Sorry about that.

Respectfully,

U.S. DEPARTMENT OF HOMELAND APOLOGY
MISTAKES WERE MADE
2001 · 2009

THE PEOPLE OF DARFUR
C/O PRESIDENT OMAR HASSAN AL-BASHIR
PEOPLE'S PALACE
PO BOX 281
KHARTOUM, SUDAN

AFFIX
POSTAGE
HERE

THE DIXIE CHICKS

c/o Sony Music Entertainment, Inc.
550 Madison Ave.
New York, NY 10022-3211

Dear Chicks,

On March 10, 2003, you were performing in London when your lead singer, Natalie Maines, proclaimed, "We're ashamed that the president of the United States is from Texas."

Not exactly a sentiment you'd expect to hear between songs like "Cowboy Take Me Away" and "Travelin' Soldier."

We all know what happened next. Your sales tanked. Your albums were rounded up and crushed by angry "fans." Country radio boycotted you. One station in Colorado suspended two of its disc jockeys for playing your music. You were booed at your own concerts. You were booed at the Academy of Country Music Awards. You received death threats.

I am sorry you had to go through all that. But amid all the paranoid, blindly patriotic backlash, something incredible happened . . .

You became cool.

You got Rick Rubin to produce your comeback album. You got Academy Award winner Barbara Kopple to make a documentary about your blacklisting. You refused to back down from Natalie's comments. And you know what? The majority of America caught up with your way of thinking. Four years after country music threw you under the bus, you won five Grammys, including album of the year.

I'll admit, before the "incident" I wouldn't have been caught dead with one of your songs on my playlist. But now? Owning a Dixie Chicks album is kind of . . . rebellious.

And there's nothing more American than rebellion.

Yours truly,

THE DIXIE CHICKS
C/O SONY MUSIC ENTERTAINMENT, INC.
550 MADISON AVE.
NEW YORK, NY 10022-3211

DR. RICHARD CARMONA
c/o Canyon Ranch
8600 E. Rockcliff Rd.
Tucson, Arizona 85750

Dear Dr. Carmona,

As surgeon general from 2002 to 2006, you were particularly dedicated to the fight against obesity and secondhand smoke. Unfortunately, the Bush administration was equally dedicated to keeping you silent on other issues, such as stem-cell research and global warming.

On July 10, 2007, you told Congress that the administration had pressured you against speaking your mind on these and other topics:

"Anything that doesn't fit into the political appointees' ideological, theological, or political agenda is ignored, marginalized, or simply buried."

You also told Congress that you'd been ordered to mention the president three times per page during speeches (this revelation finally explains your scandalous 2004 lecture, "President Bush's Bushy Presidential Bush").

I'm sorry, Dr. Carmona. Apparently your medical opinion—formed through years of experience as a paramedic, physician, professor of surgery, and hospital administrator— was less important than sparing the president's political base the horror of seeing paraplegics get up and walk.

I guess miracle cures belong to Jesus.

Best,

U.S. DEPARTMENT OF HOMELAND APOLOGY

AFFIX
POSTAGE
HERE

DR. RICHARD CARMONA
C/O CANYON RANCH
8600 E. ROCKCLIFF RD.
TUCSON, ARIZONA 85750

PRES. GEORGE H. W. BUSH
c/o George Bush Presidential Library and Museum
1000 George Bush Drive West
College Station, TX 77845

Dear Mr. President,

Let me first congratulate you on having your name appear *three times* in one mailing address. Quite an accomplishment, indeed.

Sir, I write to offer my deepest condolences. Other than siring two of your grandchildren and giving you a lovely daughter-in-law, your son George has never been much cause for celebration. There were the early days of alcoholism and alleged cocaine use. The drunk driving arrest; the cheerleading. There was his failed attempt at running an oil company. His failed attempt at running a baseball team. And his failed attempt at running the world.

When asked if he consulted you before going to war, your son told Bob Woodward, "He is the wrong father to appeal to for advice. . . . There's a higher father that I appeal to."

I can only imagine how heartbreaking that was. After all, you've always done your best. Given him every opportunity to succeed. You got him into Yale, where he barely scraped by. You got him out of going to Vietnam. You pretended to love him as much as you love Jeb. And how did he thank you? How did he reward you for all the privilege and opportunity you lavished upon him? By sullying your good name, sir.

Generations from now, when people think of George Bush, what will come to mind? Your valiant service as a fighter pilot in WWII? Your prescient decision not to get bogged down in an occupation of Iraq during the first Gulf War?

No. They'll picture your son parading around in a flight suit.

If only he'd appealed to a different father for advice.

Yours truly,

U.S. DEPARTMENT OF HOMELAND APOLOGY · MISTAKES WERE MADE · 2001 2009

PRES. GEORGE H. W. BUSH
C/O GEORGE BUSH PRESIDENTIAL LIBRARY AND MUSEUM
1000 GEORGE BUSH DRIVE WEST
COLLEGE STATION, TX 77845

THE ENGLISH LANGUAGE

c/o Harvard University Department of English
and American Literature and Language
Barker Center
12 Quincy St.
Cambridge, MA 02138

Dear English Language,

Where does I begins? (Sorry, just trying to break the ice.)

No individual, with the possible exception of Larry the Cable Guy, has wronged you so profoundly. Injured you so audaciously. Wielded you with such a lack of profundity.

Many of George W. Bush's seemingly endless verbal gaffes are, by now, known to most of the You-speaking world. There's his timeless "is our children learning?" His show-stopping "misunderestimated" and "uninalienable rights." And of course, his butchering of the old "fool me once, shame on you" axiom. Classics, all.

And let's not forget the "nuke-u-ler" issue. Which raises some important questions:

As the de facto leaders of the free world—with the fury of a nuke-u-ler arsenal at their fingertips—shouldn't our presidents be held to a standard of linguistic excellence? At the very least, shouldn't they be able to communicate effectively? If for no other reason than the fact that they're supposed to represent the best of what America has to offer?

What's a schoolchild supposed to think when the holder of our nation's highest office has such poor speaking skills? Where's the incentive to broaden one's vocabulary if the verbally inept can become president? And for crying out loud, wasn't his wife a librarian?

God, I miss Dan Quayle.

Sinceriliously,

U.S. DEPARTMENT OF HOMELAND APOLOGY

2001 · 2009

MISTAKES WERE MADE

THE ENGLISH LANGUAGE
C/O HARVARD UNIVERSITY DEPARTMENT OF ENGLISH
AND AMERICAN LITERATURE AND LANGUAGE
BARKER CENTER
12 QUINCY ST.
CAMBRIDGE, MA 02138

VICE PRESIDENT DAN QUAYLE
Cerberus Capital Management, L.P.
299 Park Ave.
New York, NY 10171

Dear Vice President Quayle,

On July 14, 2006, you were at a John Mellencamp concert when Mr. Mellencamp (unaware that you were in the audience) dedicated the song "Walk Tall" to "all the poor people who've been ignored by the current administration." You immediately stormed out, deciding that (according to your spokesman) "enough was enough."

Mr. Quayle, I'm sorry you were subjected to that kind of hate speech. Questioning one's government is simply un-American, and I applaud your refusal to tolerate it. I also understand why you're so protective of George W. Bush.

Until he came along, you were in danger of being remembered as the dumbest man in White House history.

You say potatoe,

P.S.: You still have a spokesman? Seriously?

U.S. DEPARTMENT OF HOMELAND APOLOGY

2001 · 2009 · MISTAKES WERE MADE

VICE PRESIDENT DAN QUAYLE
CERBERUS CAPITAL MANAGEMENT, L.P.
299 PARK AVE.
NEW YORK, NY 10171

VICE PRESIDENT AL GORE
The Alliance for Climate Protection
120 Hawthorne Ave.
Palo Alto, CA 94301

Dear Vice President Gore,

I'm sorry the Supreme Court decided to go with the other guy. But in hindsight, the "other guy" may have gotten the short end of the stick. Let's compare your accomplishments since the 2000 election:

You: Won the Nobel Peace Prize. Won an Emmy. Won an Academy Award. Started a TV network. Organized a landmark concert event. Wrote a #1 best seller. Became a professor. Became an advisor to companies such as Apple and Google. Launched an investment firm. Made lots and lots and lots of money. Became the world's leading voice on climate change.

The other guy: Referred to the president of Russia as "Pootie-Poot."

So, don't forget to put stamps on those thank-you cards. And, remember, there's only one "l" in "Scalia."

Very truly yours,

U.S. DEPARTMENT OF HOMELAND APOLOGY
MISTAKES WERE MADE · 2001 · 2009

VICE PRESIDENT AL GORE
THE ALLIANCE FOR CLIMATE PROTECTION
120 HAWTHORNE AVE.
PALO ALTO, CA 94301

AFRICAN AMERICANS
c/o NAACP
4805 Mt. Hope Dr.
Baltimore, MD 21215

Dear African Americans,

I'd like to apologize.

During his first term, George W. Bush became the first president since Warren G. Harding to avoid addressing the NAACP. When asked to characterize his relationship with the organization, he called it "basically nonexistent."

But that's not why I'm apologizing.

During a meeting with the Congressional Black Caucus, the president said that he was "unfamiliar" with the Voting Rights Act of 1965, a Civil Rights milestone and one of the most important acts of legislation in American history.

That's not why I'm apologizing either.

The assault on affirmative action? More black men in prison than in college? Playing on racial tensions in the 2000 primaries? Katrina?

Nope.

During his second term, an NBC/Wall Street Journal poll gave the president a job approval rating of 2 percent among African Americans—the lowest ever recorded.

I'm apologizing for the 2 percent of you who were failed by America's education system.

All the best,

U.S. DEPARTMENT OF HOMELAND APOLOGY

2001 · 2009 · MISTAKES WERE MADE

AFFIX
POSTAGE
HERE

AFRICAN AMERICANS
C/O NAACP
4805 MT. HOPE DR.
BALTIMORE, MD 21215

DEAN KAMEN
DEKA Research & Development Corp.
340 Commercial St. #401
Manchester, NH 03101

Dear Mr. Kamen,

In June 2003, President Bush attempted to mount one of your Segway personal transporters. In doing so, he tripped and nearly fell. The incident was captured by a photographer and published around the world, leading some to believe that the device was difficult to use, even dangerous.

Having ridden one myself, I know that nothing could be further from the truth. Not only is the Segway easy to use, it's remarkably tough to tip over. If I had to guess, I'd say that was because of the five gyroscopic sensors, two accelerometers, and numerous microprocessors devoted to keeping it upright at all times. Come to think of it, you'd have to be clumsier than a three-legged giraffe to fall off one of those things.

Anyway, sorry if the president cost you any potential revenue. But hey, you're extremely wealthy, so he probably made it up to you in massive tax breaks.

Best,

DEAN KAMEN
DEKA RESEARCH & DEVELOPMENT CORP.
340 SOMMERCIAL ST. #401
MANCHESTER, NH 03101

MR. MICHAEL MOORE
Dog Eat Dog Films
PO Box 831
Radio City Station
New York, NY 10101

Dear Mike,

Remember the 75th annual Academy Awards? Allow me to refresh your memory:

After winning best documentary feature for *Bowling for Columbine* (congratulations, by the way), you said the following: "We live in a time where we have a man sending us to war for fictitious reasons." You continued to a mix of cheers and boos: "We are against this war, Mr. Bush! Shame on you, Mr. Bush!"

Now, I'll admit, I was a tad annoyed with you that night, Mike.

You have to remember, this was five days after the start of the war. We'd been told that Saddam posed a direct threat to our well-being. We'd been told he was complicit in the events of 9/11. We'd been told he was trying to acquire "significant quantities of uranium from Africa." Holy shit! What were we waiting for? Kick his ass and take his gas! U-S-A! U-S-A!

And here was Michael Moore—darling of the Hollywood liberals—using the biggest stage in the world to criticize our president. Um, excuse me, did you not see Colin Powell's presentation to the UN? Were you not listening when the vice president said that "we believe [Saddam] has, in fact, reconstituted nuclear weapons" one week earlier?

Listen, Mike, I'm not perfect, OK? It was just . . . the whole thing was just so exciting, you know? What with the shock and the awe. I guess I just got so wrapped up in the flag waving that my thinking cap fell off. I mean, five days into the whole mess, and you were right. Not just right, but unafraid to say it. That takes balls. I'm sorry I forgot to question my leaders, Mike. And I'm sorry I (and others) shouted you down for being a dissenter. It won't happen again.

Sincerely,

U.S. DEPARTMENT OF HOMELAND APOLOGY · MISTAKES WERE MADE · 2001 2009

MR. MICHAEL MOORE
DOG EAT DOG FILMS
PO BOX 831
RADIO CITY STATION
NEW YORK, NY 10101

MR. HARRY M. WHITTINGTON
807 Brazos St. Suite 1010
Austin, TX 78701

Dear Mr. Whittington,

I'm sorry Dick Cheney shot you in the face.

Sincerely,

U.S. DEPARTMENT OF HOMELAND APOLOGY

AFFIX
POSTAGE
HERE

MR. HARRY M. WHITTINGTON
807 BRAZOS ST. SUITE 1010
AUSTIN, TX 78701

JESUS CHRIST™
c/o National Association of Evangelicals
PO Box 23269
Washington, DC 20026

Dear Jesus,

I dig you, man. But it seems like every time someone uses your name lately, they're talking about how much they hate somebody.

See, for the longest time, there was only the Old Testament. You know, plagues, floods, earthquakes, and such. I'm not gonna lie, Jesus. It was a real downer.

But then You came along. And just like that, we had the New Testament! New and improved, filled with lessons of love, brotherhood, charity, peace, and above all forgiveness. Do unto others as you would have them do unto you. Let he who is without sin cast the first stone. Love your enemies as you love yourself.

What a beautiful way to live. What a beautiful world you described. And what did we do? We let you down and sent you packing.

It's been a long time since you walked the earth, and people seem to have forgotten what you were all about. Nowadays, some folks use you as a basis to exclude rather than to reach out. Persecute rather than forgive. Hate rather than love. They use their "faith" in you to attack immigrants and gays. They use your "message" to promote wars and erode the separation of church and state. It pains me to say it, Jesus, but the president of the United States is one of those people.

Is that what you were driving at? Really? Hate those unlike yourself? Condemn thy neighbor? Make me a political football?

I refuse to believe it. That's not the Jesus I know and love.

Sorry, man. I guess we let you down again.

Yours in You,

U.S. DEPARTMENT OF HOMELAND APOLOGY

JESUS CHRIST™
C/O NATIONAL ASSOCIATION OF EVANGELICALS
PO BOX 23269
WASHINGTON, DC 20026

L'Oréal USA
Attn: Laurent Attal, President and CEO
575 Fifth Ave.
New York, NY 10017

Dear L'Oréal,

I'd like to apologize to you and the rest of the cosmetics industry for the physical appearance of Katherine Harris, George W. Bush's close friend and ally who helped him win the contested presidential race in the state of Florida in 2000.

While millions of women use your products safely and responsibly, an unfortunate few abuse them in vile and disgusting ways.

However, just as we cannot ban alcohol simply because of drunk drivers, nor can we dispose of grocery stores because of the morbidly obese, we cannot and should not ban the sale of cosmetics on account of those who choose to embody the question: What would the Joker look like if he dressed as a whore for Halloween?

May God bless your products and all the innocent faces they adhere to.

Colorfully,

U.S. DEPARTMENT OF HOMELAND APOLOGY
MISTAKES WERE MADE
2001 2009

L'ORÉAL USA
ATTN: LAURENT ATTAL, PRESIDENT AND CEO
575 FIFTH AVE.
NEW YORK, NY 10017

WOMEN
c/o The National Organization for Women
1100 H St. NW, 3rd Floor
Washington, DC 20005

Dear Women,

I'm writing to apologize on behalf of President George W. Bush.

During his first days in office, he disbanded the President's Integrity Council on Women, which had been created by Bill Clinton in 1995 to ensure that policies were fair to both genders. He issued a global gag rule preventing overseas family-planning clinics from suggesting abortion as an alternative, even in parts of Africa where one in sixteen women dies during pregnancy. He pushed to roll back parts of Title IX, which bans gender discrimination in college sports. Through policy, judicial appointments, and legislation, his administration consistently attacked reproductive rights.

Hmm, for someone with so many women in his life, he sure doesn't want them to have much say in theirs.

Hopefully, some future president will come in and clean house, ridding it of the antiquated idea that the government knows what's better for a woman than her doctor. Who knows? Maybe that president will be a woman.

After all, nobody cleans a house better than a woman. Wait! No, wait—I meant, if you want *a* clean house—no, *to* clean house—

Oh, forget it.

Femininely,

U.S. DEPARTMENT OF HOMELAND APOLOGY

MISTAKES WERE MADE · 2001 · 2009

WOMEN
C/O THE NATIONAL ORGANIZATION FOR WOMEN
1100 H ST. NW, 3RD FLOOR
WASHINGTON, DC 20005

AMERICAN CHILDREN
c/o Save the Children
54 Wilton Rd.
Westport, CT 06880

Dear American Children,

Hi! Do you like living in America? Me, too! I like all sorts of things about America! A lot of those things begin with the letter "F," like freedom, family, football, the Fourth of July, and fast food. But do you know what else begins with the letter "F"?

Failure. Do you know what "failure" is?

Failure is the fact that nine million of you can't afford to go to the doctor if you get sick or bump your noodle (ouch!). The U.S. Congress tried super-duper hard to get health insurance for some of you. For once, they stopped fighting like poopy faces and learned to share. But then, a man named President Bush vetoed the law (that means he tore it up and went number one on it)! Boy, he sure sounds like a mean ol' crankypuss!

Failure also means that 13 million of you don't have enough money or enough to eat or warm clothes in wintertime. Did you know that 17 percent of all the kids in America live in poverty? You did? Very good! Did you know that 150,000 of you have become poor every year since President Bush took office? What a nasty chicken-nugget head!

But do you want to know the biggest failure of them all? No, not the disastrous war in Iraq. No, not the explosion of hatred for America around the world. No, not the back-breaking national debt that you'll be paying off for the rest of your lives.

It's President Bush!

He gets an "F" for being president! Does that mean he gets a do-over? Gee, I sure hope not. Then we'd all have to kill ourselves! Hooray!

Giggles and gumdrops,

U.S. DEPARTMENT OF HOMELAND APOLOGY
2001 · MISTAKES WERE MADE · 2009

AMERICAN CHILDREN
C/O SAVE THE CHILDREN
54 WILTON RD.
WESTPORT, CT 06880

MR. WILLIAM K. HAMPTON
Leon County Jail
Housing Pod K
535 Appleyard Dr.
Tallahassee, FL 32304

Dear Mr. Hampton,

On January 20, 2001, Mr. Kenneth Wayne Cooper, your fellow inmate, was charged with beating the crap out of you. Why? For expressing happiness that George W. Bush was headed for the White House.

Look, I'm not crazy about Bush, but nobody deserves an ass-whooping for supporting him. Not even Ron Silver, who's a Jew from Manhattan and ought to know better.

Please accept my deepest apologies.

Sincerely,

U.S. DEPARTMENT OF HOMELAND APOLOGY · MISTAKES WERE MADE · 2001 2009

MR. WILLIAM K. HAMPTON
LEON COUNTY JAIL
HOUSING POD K
535 APPLEYARD DR.
TALLAHASSEE, FL 32304

SADDAM HUSSEIN
c/o Embassy of the United States
APO AE 09316
Baghdad, Iraq

Saddam,

Boy, am I glad you're dead! Let's see: You gassed thousands of innocent men, women, and children. You used torture, kidnapping, and mass murder as a means of intimidation. You executed your own family members, beheaded hundreds of women, and lived like a sultan while your people starved. And, from what I've seen of your palaces, you had terrible taste. The world is a much better place without you. If you'll excuse my saying so, you were a total a-hole.

That said . . .

It would've been nice if you'd been deposed for something you actually did. I mean, after all the horrible, despicable atrocities you committed, it was ultimately a trumped-up charge that broke the camel's back. (No, Mr. Hussein, not an actual camel—it's a Western saying.)

Nailing you on WMDs was the equivalent of executing Jeffrey Dahmer for unpaid parking tickets. I mean, sure—I'm glad you got him—but where were you when he was stocking his fridge with severed heads?

Hang loose,

U.S. DEPARTMENT OF HOMELAND APOLOGY
2001 · 2009
MISTAKES WERE MADE

SADDAM HUSSEIN
C/O EMBASSY OF THE UNITED STATES
APO AE 09316
BAGHDAD, IRAQ

GAY REPUBLICANS
c/o Log Cabin Republicans
1901 Pennsylvania Ave. NW, Suite 902
Washington, DC 20006

Dear Gay Republicans,

What a fabulous mess these last eight years have been.

Believe it or not, the term *gay Republican* wasn't always an oxymoron. Thanks in large part to your fighting, in the 1990s the GOP had gone a long way toward being more inclusive. But that all changed in January 2001.

Most of you are members of the Republican Party because you believe in smaller government, fiscal responsibility, and personal freedoms. Under President Bush, you watched freedoms erode, government expand, and spending run wild.

You watched the president use gay marriage as a wedge issue to ignite the passions of his largely antigay base. You watched him nominate for surgeon general Dr. James Holsinger Jr., who has said that homosexuality isn't "natural or healthy." You endured the insufferable hypocrisy of fellow Republicans like Larry Craig and Mark Foley. And, worst of all, you watched the radical right complete its hijacking of your party.

I'm sorry. It looks like you've still got a lot of fighting to do.

Inclusively,

U.S. DEPARTMENT OF HOMELAND APOLOGY

2001 · 2009

MISTAKES WERE MADE

GAY REPUBLICANS
C/O LOG CABIN REPUBLICANS
1901 PENNSYLVANIA AVE. NW, SUITE 902
WASHINGTON, DC 20006

SEN. LARRY CRAIG
520 Hart Senate Office Bldg.
Washington, DC 20510

Dear Senator Craig,

On June 11, 2007, you were arrested after allegedly soliciting sex from an undercover police officer in an airport bathroom. In August, news of the arrest became public, creating a media firestorm. You told reporters: "I am not gay. I never have been gay." But men like David Phillips, Mike Jones, Greg Ruth, and Tom Russell disagreed and began to come forward with stories of sexual encounters they'd had with you over the years.

I want to apologize, Senator. Because if you *are* gay (and for the sake of argument, let's pretend you are), then life probably hasn't been all that much fun. What a heavy, ceaseless burden it must be to carry all those lies around. To live in the shadows. But worse—so much worse than any of that—what crippling shame you must feel.

I know how much it must've tortured you to vote for a proposed constitutional amendment to ban gay marriage and against a bill to ban discrimination on the basis of sexual orientation. I wonder, Senator, what made you graduate from closet case to hypocrite? Was it that self-loathing voice that's always told you how sinful, vile, and disgusting those urges were? I wonder, was it that same voice that made Republican Congressman Mark Foley call rumors that he was gay "revolting and unforgivable" or that convinced evangelical pastor Ted Haggard to preach against homosexuality?

I can't imagine how hard it must be to go through life like that. Thinking so little of yourself. Forced to find cheap thrills in airport bathrooms instead of being free to feel the warmth of true companionship. I pity you, Senator. Really.

Just promise me one thing: If you ever feel the urge to cruise for gay sex again, no more airport bathrooms, OK? I mean, you've got half of the Republican party to choose from.

Proudly,

U.S. DEPARTMENT OF HOMELAND APOLOGY

SEN. LARRY CRAIG
520 HART SENATE OFFICE BLDG.
WASHINGTON, DC 20510

THE PEOPLE OF IRAQ
c/o Embassy of the United States
APO AE 09316
Baghdad, Iraq

Dear People of Iraq,

What can I possibly say?

I know it hasn't been easy being occupied. Having your doors kicked in. Seeing your men stripped naked and photographed for amusement. Living in constant fear of death.

On the other hand, it hasn't exactly been a picnic occupying you. How are we supposed to react when we see innocent contractors kidnapped and beheaded? When we see the charred bodies of American civilians paraded through the streets? Would you prefer we just packed up and left? Would you rather we let your completely ineffectual government handle things? Should we leave you to enjoy a few decades of civil war or prop up another brutal dictator and let him have his way with you?

I'm sorry things turned out the way they have. I'm sorry George W. Bush chose you as the subject for his experiment in preemptive war. I'm sorry we didn't send enough troops to secure the peace. I'm sorry we botched restoring basic services like electricity. But all the apologies in the world won't change that we are where we are. No apology can bring back the thousands of Americans who have been killed or maimed on your streets, or the tens of thousands of you who have died since the invasion.

We don't want to be in Iraq any more than you want us to be in Iraq. You think American soldiers enjoy being in your country? Have you ever been to America? Let me tell you, it's way, way more fun than Iraq.

You want us to leave? It's very simple:

Get your shit together.

All the best,

AFFIX
POSTAGE
HERE

THE PEOPLE OF IRAQ
C/O EMBASSY OF THE UNITED STATES
APO AE 09316
BAGHDAD, IRAQ

FAMILY VALUES

c/o American Family Association
PO Drawer 2440
Tupelo, MS 38803

Dear Family Values,

George W. Bush has spent a lot of time telling us what kinds of values our families should adhere to. I thought it'd be fun to take a look at the values embraced by his family:

His grandpa, Prescott Bush, was one of the directors of Union Banking Corp., which was controlled by a financial backer of Adolf Hitler.

His brother Neil divorced his wife of twenty-two years after an affair, and he admitted he'd had sex with "three or four" women during their marriage, including escorts in Thailand. This is the same Neil who was sued after the collapse of Silverado Banking (which has cost taxpayers about $1 billion to bail out).

And then there's Jeb's family. Jeb's wife, Columba, was caught trying to sneak $19,000 worth of clothing and jewelry into the United States after a Paris shopping spree. His daughter Noelle was arrested for trying to pass a fake prescription for Xanax, and his son George broke into an ex-girlfriend's Miami home and drove his SUV across her lawn. His other son John was arrested for public intoxication and resisting arrest.

Even the president has admitted to being quite the hard-partying youth—if by "youth" you mean "thirty years old," his age when he was arrested for drunk driving.

So there you go. Driving drunk, getting high, breaking and entering, screwing investors, cheating on wives, smuggling, fraud, and funding Nazis: Bush family values.

I can't imagine that having such a brazen hypocrite for a spokesperson has been good for business, Family Values. So allow me to offer a sincere apology for the past eight years.

Yours truly,

U.S. DEPARTMENT OF HOMELAND APOLOGY

2001 2009
MISTAKES WERE MADE

AFFIX
POSTAGE
HERE

FAMILY VALUES
C/O AMERICAN FAMILY ASSOCIATION
PO DRAWER 2440
TUPELO, MS 38803

GEN. COLIN POWELL (RET.)

c/o America's Promise Alliance
909 N. Washington St., Suite 400
Alexandria, VA 22314

Dear General Powell,

On February 5, 2003, you addressed the UN Security Council, claiming that "there can be no doubt that Saddam Hussein has biological weapons and the capability to rapidly produce more." You cited eyewitness accounts of mobile weapons labs, suggested a partnership between Iraq and Al Qaeda, and spoke of the impending nuclear threat posed by Saddam. You submitted—in no uncertain terms—that Iraq was a direct and dire threat to America. "My colleagues, every statement I make today is backed up by sources, solid sources. These are not assertions. What we're giving you are facts and conclusions based on solid intelligence." Your words.

It was a galvanizing moment on the road to war. Too bad none of it was true.

In fact, some of the "facts" in your presentation had been plagiarized from an essay by a graduate student.

Behind the scenes, you had pleaded with the president not to invade Iraq, but he'd already made up his mind. And when it came time to sell his case to the world, he chose you—no doubt because of your popularity with the American public and credibility on the world stage. And, ever the good soldier, you obliged.

You're owed an apology, General. The UN debacle is a blight on an otherwise exemplary record. A blight that I believe you were unknowingly led into.

Respectfully,

GEN. COLIN POWELL (RET.)
C/O AMERICA'S PROMISE ALLIANCE
909 N. WASHINGTON ST., SUITE 400
ALEXANDRIA, VA 22314

ABSTINENT TEENS
c/o True Love Waits
One LifeWay Plaza
Nashville, TN 37234

Dear Abstinent Teens,

I'm guessing most of the millions of you who've taken an "abstinence pledge" are big fans of President Bush. Well, he's a big fan of yours, too. His administration has given hundreds of millions of dollars to programs that encourage kids to keep their junk in a lock box until they walk down the aisle.

But your purity comes at a price. Statistically speaking, you're more likely to engage in anal and oral sex than teens who don't take "the pledge" and less likely to use condoms. (I guess it's no surprise that you have similar rates of sexually transmitted diseases.) A report in the *American Journal of Public Health* found that 53 percent of you deny ever taking the pledge one year after having taken it (presumably because you've already broken it). A 2007 study mandated by congress found that you were just as likely to have sex before marriage as non-pledge teens.

Do me a favor: You want to save yourself for Prince Charming or Princess Goldenhole? Great. I applaud you. But don't use abstinence as an excuse for ignorance. Instead of those ridiculous pledge rings that companies are getting rich selling you, go buy a box of condoms before your next all-night session of "doesn't count as real sex" anal and oral.

You'll be a lot safer, and your future spouse will thank you for sparing him/her the raging case of genital warts.

Purely,

U.S. DEPARTMENT OF HOMELAND APOLOGY

MISTAKES WERE MADE

2001 2009

AFFIX
POSTAGE
HERE

ABSTINENT TEENS
C/O TRUE LOVE WAITS
ONE LIFEWAY PLAZA
NASHVILLE, TN 37234

THE BUCK

c/o Harry S. Truman Library and Museum
500 W. U.S. Hwy. 24
Independence, MO 64050

Dear Buck,

President Harry Truman used to have a small wooden sign on his desk that read "The Buck Stops Here," a take on the old expression "pass the buck," meaning "let somebody else deal with it." Truman kept it as a reminder that a president has to accept responsibility for the decisions of his administration.

On April 13, 2004, President George W. Bush was asked to name one mistake he'd made since taking office. His reply:

"I'm sure something will pop into my head here in the midst of this press conference, with all the pressure of trying to come up with answer, but it hadn't yet."

That's right: He couldn't come up with a single one. After ignoring warnings about Al Qaeda striking America, waging a disastrous war of choice, and standing under a "Mission Accomplished" banner while soldiers were dying, the man couldn't think of a single thing he'd done wrong.

Sorry, Buck. The president's desk used to be a place to rest up and catch your breath. But from the sound of things, you haven't stopped in years.

Responsibly,

U.S. DEPARTMENT OF HOMELAND APOLOGY · WE'RE MADE MISTAKES · 2009 · 2001

AFFIX
POSTAGE
HERE

THE BUCK
C/O HARRY S. TRUMAN LIBRARY AND MUSEUM
500 W. U.S. HWY. 24
INDEPENDENCE, MO 64050

OSAMA BIN LADEN
c/o Central Intelligence Agency
Office of Public Affairs
Washington, DC 20505

Mr. Bin Laden,

I'm sorry we haven't gotten around to killing you yet, but it's time you knew why.

Remember the caves of Tora Bora, where, according to a CIA officer, we had you pinned back in December 2001? Remember how you were able to escape because our military wouldn't send the extra troops the CIA requested?

Now let me ask you: Do you think that was a mistake? Do you think the United States of America—with its special forces, spy satellites, UAVs, and intelligence-gathering capabilities—can't find one sickly, freakishly tall multimillionaire with whom it once enjoyed close ties? I mean, honestly, Mr. Bin Laden.

Truth is, you've been a pawn in the most successful covert mission in history: "Operation Make More Terrorists," an ingenuous strategy drawn up by America's top minds on the morning of September 12, 2001. Its five objectives:

- Fail to capture Bin Laden at all costs, allowing him to achieve mythic status.
- Invade a Middle Eastern country with no ties to 9/11.
- Wait until 2005, then disband the CIA unit assigned to capturing Bin Laden.
- ?
- Win the war on terror.

Now, can you imagine what would've happened if we'd killed you at Tora Bora a scant two months after September 11, 2001? Or if we'd focused our military might on Afghanistan instead of hunting for make-believe WMDs in Iraq?

Exactly. It would've been a catastrophe. But fear not, Mr. Bin Laden. As of this writing, you're in your early fifties. Considering your health problems, family history, and lifestyle, I give you another thirty or forty years, tops. So take that.

Just keep livin',

U.S. DEPARTMENT OF HOMELAND APOLOGY
MISTAKES WERE MADE
2001 2009

OSAMA BIN LADEN
C/O CENTRAL INTELLIGENCE AGENCY
OFFICE OF PUBLIC AFFAIRS
WASHINGTON, DC 20505

THE MIDDLE CLASS
c/o Communities United to Strengthen America
1050 17th St. NW, Suite 830
Washington, DC 20036

Dear Middle Class,

In February 2005, George W. Bush was in Omaha, Nebraska, to promote his doomed Social Security plan. Chatting with the audience, he met Mary Mornin, a divorced mother of three who told the president she worked three jobs. He seemed astonished. What sort of solace would he offer her? What words of support? How would he use this case as the perfect example of why the minimum wage hike was long overdue? "Uniquely American, isn't it?" he replied. "I mean, that is fantastic that you're doing that." The audience erupted in brainless applause.

That's the way Bush views your struggles, Middle Class. "Uniquely American." Need two full-time incomes just to get by? Uniquely American. Seen your job go overseas? Uniquely American. Have your retirement fund looted by corporate fat cats? Working harder to earn less? Finding it impossible to keep up with healthcare premiums (which have risen more than 80 percent since 2000) or gas prices (which have more than doubled since Bush took office)?

Uniquely American.

And the president further displayed his admiration for your uniqueness by shifting the tax burden off the backs of the wealthiest Americans—and onto yours. Losing more than three million American manufacturing jobs since he took office. Refusing to enforce fair trade with China. Cutting taxes on capital gains and dividends (which mostly benefit the rich) while you watched your median household incomes shrink.

I'm sorry, Middle Class. I guess that's the price you pay for being different.

All the best,

U.S. DEPARTMENT OF HOMELAND APOLOGY
2001 · MISTAKES WERE MADE · 2009

THE MIDDLE CLASS
C/O COMMUNITIES UNITED TO STRENGTHEN AMERICA
1050 17TH ST. NW, SUITE 830
WASHINGTON, DC 20036

PRETZELS
c/o The Snack Food Association
1600 Wilson Blvd., Suite 650
Arlington, VA 22209

Dear Pretzels,

In January 2002, President George W. Bush lost consciousness and collapsed after choking on one of your brethren.

In the subsequent media firestorm, you were portrayed as attempted murderers. Would-be assassins. Millions of you were ripped from your bags and stomped in the streets. Fly-by-night psychologists suggested that your twisted shape bore a resemblance to your state of mind. Your ever-present nemesis, the potato chip, took cheap jabs at your German heritage, going so far as to call you "salted Hitlers."

However, it was soon revealed that the president choked not because you tried to kill him but because he neglected to chew you before swallowing. He has since learned that this step is an important part of the eating process.

Pretzels, America owes you an apology.

Sincerely,

PRETZELS

C/O THE SNACK FOOD ASSOCIATION

1600 WILSON BLVD., SUITE 650

ARLINGTON, VA 22209

AFFIX
POSTAGE
HERE

GEN. ERIC SHINSEKI (RET.)
Grove Farm Company Inc.
3-1850 Kaumualii Hwy.
Lihue, HI 96766-7069

Dear General Shinseki,

As a four-star general and army chief of staff, you appeared before the Senate Armed Services Committee on February 25, 2003, just days before the start of the Iraq War.

When asked how many troops it would take to secure the peace after an invasion, you told the senators "several hundred thousand."

"We're talking about post-hostilities control over a piece of geography that's fairly significant, with the kinds of ethnic tensions that could lead to other problems. And so it takes a significant ground-force presence."

Three days later, Deputy Secretary of Defense Paul Wolfowitz told the House Budget Committee that your estimates were "outlandish" and "wildly off the mark."

But Wolfowitz wasn't the only bigwig to jump on the Shinseki-bashing bus. One senior Pentagon official told a reporter that your estimate was "bullshit from a Clintonite enamored of using the army for peacekeeping and not winning wars."

Four years after your testimony, with Iraq an absolute disaster, the president decided to try a so-called surge in troop levels (though nowhere near those you suggested). As of this writing, it seems to be helping.

I'm sorry it took him so long to agree with you, General. I wonder how many lives could've been saved if he'd listened to you in the first place.

With respect,

AFFIX
POSTAGE
HERE

GEN. ERIC SHINSEKI (RET.)
GROVE FARM COMPANY INC.
3-1850 KAUMUALII HWY.
LIHUE, HI 96766-7069

PRESIDENT FIDEL CASTRO
c/o Cuban Interests Section
2639 16th St. NW
Washington, DC 20009

President Castro,

On July 16, 2004, President George W. Bush accused you of "welcoming" sex tourism in Cuba. To back up this claim, he quoted you as saying: "Cuba has the cleanest and most educated prostitutes in the world." It was a damning accusation, one that made it all the more clear why the United States refused to have anything to do with Cuba so long as you were in power.

That is, until the *Los Angeles Times* discovered that the quote was lifted from a Dartmouth student's paper and that you'd been (a) misquoted and (b) misquoted out of context. During a speech in 1992, you did remark that although prostitution still existed in Cuba, the women had more schooling and a much lower rate of HIV than prostitutes in other parts of the world (another glorious benefit of your revolution, no doubt). In fact, you outlawed prostitution when you came to power in 1959.

Please accept my apology, Mr. President. You are many things, but apparently a whore-monger isn't one of them.

Viva la prostitución,

P.S.: Hope my retirement card arrived OK.

PRESIDENT FIDEL CASTRO
C/O CUBAN INTERESTS SECTION
2639 16TH ST. NW
WASHINGTON, DC 20009

THE WORD "ACCOMPLISHED"
c/o Merriam-Webster, Inc.
47 Federal St.
PO Box 281
Springfield, MA 01102

Dear "Accomplished,"

You used to be a delightful adjective meaning "completed, done, or established beyond doubt or dispute."

Then somebody hung you on an aircraft carrier.

Now you mean "bogged down in the middle of someone else's civil war."

Sorry.

Sincerely,

U.S. DEPARTMENT OF HOMELAND APOLOGY
MISTAKES WERE MADE
2001 2009

THE WORD "ACCOMPLISHED"
C/O MERRIAM-WEBSTER, INC.
47 FEDERAL ST.
PO BOX 281
SPRINGFIELD, MA 01102

MR. PAUL O'NEILL
The Blackstone Group
345 Park Ave.
New York, NY 10154

Dear Mr. O'Neill

Hey, remember when you worked as George W. Bush's Treasury secretary during the first two years of his administration? In 2001 you stood by the president when (in a rare case of fulfilling a campaign promise) he pushed through a $1 trillion cut aimed at the wealthiest 1 percent of Americans.

The following year, with our nation at war, the administration decided to push for a second round of tax cuts—again aimed at the rich. You argued against it, citing the cost of the war, programs like Social Security, and the growing budget deficit. As you later told the world, Dick Cheney disagreed, pointing out that "deficits don't matter."

When you refused to publicly support the cuts, you were asked to resign.

Today, with the United States more than $9 trillion in the red, a flaccid dollar, and a federal budget deficit of $449.5 billion in 2006, it appears you're owed an apology.

But don't worry about the American economy too much, Mr. O'Neill.

Apparently, deficits don't matter.

Indebted,

U.S. DEPARTMENT OF HOMELAND APOLOGY · MISTAKES WERE MADE · 2001 2009

MR. PAUL O'NEILL
THE BLACKSTONE GROUP
345 PARK AVE.
NEW YORK, NY 10154

MR. SCOTT MCCLELLAN
HHB, Inc.
816 Connecticut Ave., 5th Floor
Washington, DC 20006

Dear Scott,

In October 2003, you stood at the podium of the White House briefing room and told the world that neither Karl Rove nor Scooter Libby had anything to do with the leak of a CIA spy's identity. You knew that was the case, since, as you stated: "Those individuals assured me they were not involved in this. And that's where it stands."

Four years later, you wrote:

"I had unknowingly passed along false information. And five of the highest-ranking officials in the administration were involved in my doing so: Rove, Libby, the vice president, the president's chief of staff, and the president himself."

Woopsie doodles.

They sold you down the Rio Grande, Scott. They bent you over and went at you like Jeff Gannon* in a nightclub bathroom. And did any of them apologize? No.

So let me do it for them: I'm sorry, Scott. You got played like a Texas fiddle in front of the whole world. But at least you learned an invaluable lesson in the process:

Never trust anything that comes out of the Bush White House.

Yours truly,

---

*If you recall, Jeff Gannon was a reporter who may or may not have been planted by the White House to ask softball questions during briefings. It eventually came out that he had little or no journalistic experience and that he once worked for a gay male escort service.

U.S. DEPARTMENT OF HOMELAND APOLOGY
2001 2009 MISTAKES WERE MADE

MR. SCOTT MCCLELLAN
HHB, INC.
816 CONNECTICUT AVE., 5TH FLOOR
WASHINGTON, DC 20006

THE ENVIRONMENT

c/o Administrator Stephen L. Johnson
U.S. Environmental Protection Agency
1200 Pennsylvania Ave. NW
Washington, DC 20460

Dear Environment,

You've looked better, Mother Nature. Remember Jodie Foster in *The Accused*? Yeah. Then again, you've been getting raped for eight years. And for that, I'm super sorry.

You must've seen it coming. After all, under Gov. George W. Bush, Texas became the most polluted state in the nation. As president, Bush called himself a "good steward of the land," and he set about proving it by suspending protection for more than 50 million acres of forests, less than three weeks into his presidency. He slashed funding for pollution cleanup, weakened endangered species protection, pushed to open Alaska's Artic Wildlife Refuge to oil drilling, pulled out of the Kyoto Treaty, and vetoed the Water Resources Development Act—which called for critical habitat restoration—because the bill "lacked fiscal discipline." This from the biggest spender in the history of our government. (Congress overrode the veto.)

And then there was the "Healthy Forests" bill, which, despite its name, actually opened 20 million acres of protected forests to logging, supposedly to "reduce the threat of destructive wildfires." In other words, if there are no more trees, we won't have any more fires (almost as brilliant as my plan to combat AIDS by getting rid of the world's blood).

But part of the blame rests with you, Mother Nature. You and I both know this never would've happened if you hadn't been so good-looking.

Kind regards,

U.S. DEPARTMENT OF HOMELAND APOLOGY · MISTAKES WERE MADE · 2001 · 2009

THE ENVIRONMENT
C/O ADMINISTRATOR STEPHEN L. JOHNSON
U.S. ENVIRONMENTAL PROTECTION AGENCY
1200 PENNSYLVANIA AVE. NW
WASHINGTON, DC 20460

MR. BILL O'REILLY
Fox News Channel
1211 Avenue of the Americas, 18th Floor
New York, NY 10036

Dear Mr. O'Reilly,

I want to apologize for all the criticism you've received from the left during the Bush presidency. Apparently, your show is simply over most liberals' heads.

I believe you're a genius, sir. And in "Bill O'Reilly," I believe you've created one of the most fully realized, iconic characters on American television. One that rivals Alf in its complexity, timeliness, and staying power.

It's no accident that *The O'Reilly Factor* (the American one) and *The Office* (the British one) are my two favorite TV shows. Both portray themselves as "real," and both revolve around men who are hilariously ignorant of how hilariously ignorant they are.

Don't your liberal critics realize that the whole thing's a put-on? I mean, can you imagine if "Bill" was a real person? Can you imagine a real anchor inviting Al Qaeda to attack a major American city? Calling Mexicans "wetbacks" on the air? Saying "I hope they're not in the parking lot stealing our hubcaps" at a fund-raiser for inner-city kids? Can you imagine someone writing a laughably terrible novel with passages like "within seconds, his tongue was inside her" and "she silently marveled at [his] stamina"? And then that same person boycotting Pepsi because its spokesperson "degrades women"?

Can you imagine what an unbelievably out-of-touch, insecure, hypocritical douchebag that guy would be?

The world of comedy owes you a debt of gratitude—and I can't wait to see what sorts of misadventures ol' Bill gets himself into in the coming seasons!

Loofah,

U.S. DEPARTMENT OF HOMELAND APOLOGY

2001 2009
MISTAKES WERE MADE

MR. BILL O'REILLY
FOX NEWS CHANNEL
1211 AVENUE OF THE AMERICAS, 18TH FLOOR
NEW YORK, NY 10036

MS. VALERIE PLAME WILSON
c/o Citizens for Responsibility and Ethics in Washington
1400 Eye St. NW, Suite 450
Washington, DC 20005

Dear Ms. Plame Wilson,

We all know that you worked for the CIA until being "outed" by America's favorite red-breasted curmudgeon, Robert Novak.

What we don't know is what you actually did for the CIA. During "Plamegate," some members of the right-wing media tried to downplay your importance. Jonah Goldberg at *The National Review* wrote: "Wilson's wife is a desk jockey, and much of the Washington cocktail circuit knew that already."

Really? A "desk jockey"? Let's go to the videotape:

You were recruited to become a CIA covert officer in 1985. You received extensive para-military training at the "farm" in Virginia. You were among the 6 percent of your class chosen to become a NOC ("knock"), or nonofficial covert agent, the deepest of the deep-cover officers who assume false identities and surrender diplomatic immunity. You used fake passports and disguises. You used automatic weapons. You were paid through a phony front company (Brewster-Jennings & Associates). You kept your real career hidden from friends and family. You served in Europe, where you were tasked with recruiting spies for the United States (on top of being wicked smart, the fact that you were wicked hot probably didn't hurt). In the late 1990s, you were placed in charge of the operations group that was looking for evidence of weapons of mass destruction in Iraq; you found nothing. I don't suppose the irony of that outcome is lost on you.

You sound more like Angelina Jolie in *Mr. and Mrs. Smith* than a "desk jockey."

Either way, I'm sorry your career was ruined, and I'm sorry that your years of service—often placing your life in danger to protect America—were largely ignored.

With sincere appreciation,

U.S. DEPARTMENT OF HOMELAND APOLOGY

2001 · MISTAKES WERE MADE · 2009

MS. VALERIE PLAME WILSON
C/O CITIZENS FOR RESPONSIBILITY AND ETHICS IN WASHINGTON
1400 EYE ST. NW, SUITE 450
WASHINGTON, DC 20005

SCIENCE
c/o National Science Teachers Association
1840 Wilson Blvd.
Arlington, VA 22201

Dear Science,

Hypothesis:

If the presence of George W. Bush in the White House is detrimental to science, then George W. Bush owes science an apology.

Observations:

Bending over backward to please creationists

Refusing to join 174 countries in signing the Kyoto Protocol to reduce carbon dioxide emissions, despite being the world's biggest polluter

Ignoring geological studies that warned of the dangers of oil exploration in the Artic National Wildlife Refuge

Overturning an FDA panel's recommendation to make "Plan B" birth control available

Opposing stem cell research for religious reasons, despite a plea from eight Nobel laureates stressing its importance

Result:

George W. Bush owes science an apology.

Conclusively,

U.S. DEPARTMENT OF HOMELAND APOLOGY

SCIENCE
C/O NATIONAL SCIENCE TEACHERS ASSOCIATION
1840 WILSON BLVD.
ARLINGTON, VA 22201

MS. HARRIET MIERS
c/o Locke Liddell & Sapp
2200 Ross Ave., Suite 2200
Dallas, TX 75201

Dear Ms. Miers,

When George W. Bush was governor of Texas, you sent him a handwritten note that said, "You are the best governor ever." Those six words were an affirmation of your love for (and loyalty to) a man you would follow from Texas to Washington.

You continued to serve him loyally through his first and second terms in your roles as staff secretary, deputy chief of staff for policy, and White House counsel.

In 2005 it seemed your loyalty was finally being rewarded. The "best president ever" nominated you to the Supreme Court (the highest court ever), but your nomination met with fervent resistance, mostly from Republicans.

So, a little more than three weeks after your nomination, you asked that your name be withdrawn. In doing so, you spared the president a long, potentially embarrassing battle with Congress, and, to protect him, you gave up your shot at a place in history.

You have kept protecting him, even after resigning from the White House. In 2007 you were cited for contempt of Congress for refusing to testify about the firings of U.S. attorneys. Later that year, it came to light that you may have known about videotapes that could've proven the CIA was conducting torture, and you had withheld this knowledge from the president, protecting him as always.

If it makes any difference, you're in good company. Quite a few people have suffered to protect him, and at least one was sentenced to prison.

You once told the president that serving him was "an impossible-to-describe privilege."

Believe me, Ms. Miers, the privilege is all his.

Sincerely,

U.S. DEPARTMENT OF
HOMELAND APOLOGY
MISTAKES WERE MADE
2001 2009

AFFIX
POSTAGE
HERE

MS. HARRIET MIERS
C/O LOCKE LIDDELL & SAPP
2200 ROSS AVE., SUITE 2200
DALLAS, TX 75201

CONSERVATIVES
c/o The Heritage Foundation
214 Massachusetts Ave. NE
Washington, DC 20002

Dear Conservatives,

Ah, the good ol' days.

The days when *conservatism* meant "smaller government," "fiscal responsibility," "uptight white people."

But that all changed when the "compassionate conservative" rode into Washington on the back of the Supreme Court. Six years after taking office, George Bush and his Republican-controlled Congress had taken those surpluses and turned them into the largest debt in the nation's history—more than $9 trillion.

While he was bleeding our coffers dry, President Bush expanded presidential powers to previously unheard-of levels and, though the Patriot Act, domestic spying, and warrant-less wiretapping, increased the invasion of government into citizens' everyday lives. He even pressed for a constitutional amendment to keep certain types of people from getting married. All in the name of "conservatism."

William F. Buckley, widely regarded as the father of your movement, doesn't label Bush a true conservative, going so far as to say: "If you had a European prime minister who experienced what we've experienced, it would be expected that he would retire or resign."

Conservative no longer means the penny-pinching, self-determining ways of your fathers and grandfathers. Thanks to Dubya, it means free-spending and big government.

But, hey, you've still got the uptight white people.

Conservatively,

U.S. DEPARTMENT OF HOMELAND APOLOGY · MISTAKES WERE MADE · 2001 2009

CONSERVATIVES
C/O THE HERITAGE FOUNDATION
214 MASSACHUSETTS AVE. NE
WASHINGTON, DC 20002

PEOPLE OF IRAN
c/o H. E. Mohammad Khazaee
Permanent Representative of Iran to the United Nations
United Nations
New York, NY 10017

Dear People of Iran,

In the words of Don Corleone, "How did things ever get so far?"

Recently, a lot has been made about out differences, so let's talk about our similarities. First, the similarities between our presidents. Both are beholden to religious extremists. Both are prone to inflammatory rhetoric. Both are largely unpopular at home.

Second, let's discuss the similarities between our citizens: I'm willing to bet that most of you just want to earn some money, spend time with your friends and family, and be left alone to squeeze whatever joy you can from this wretched existence.

Guess what—same here.

Look, you have to understand why Americans are so freaked out about you guys getting the bomb: See, the second you go nuclear, Israel's going to fly in and rain laser-guided menorahs all over you. And when they do, you're going to get all worked up, declare war on the Zionist so-and-so, and then boom, we're off to the races. You dig?

I know we fucked up your entire part of the world when we invaded Iraq. But you guys didn't exactly help matters by giving the insurgents explosives, either. You see what I'm getting at? We could blame each other till the مـرتبطکلمـات came home.

So here it is: I'm sorry for the way my leaders have behaved. But remember: Just because they feel the need to ratchet up tensions and behave like children doesn't mean we have to.

Yours in Christ,

AFFIX
POSTAGE
HERE

PEOPLE OF IRAN
C/O H. E. MOHAMMAD KHAZAEE
PERMANENT REPRESENTATIVE OF IRAN TO THE UNITED NATIONS
UNITED NATIONS
NEW YORK, NY 10017

DR. W. DAVID HAGER
1720 Nicholasville Rd., 5th Floor, Bldg. E
Lexington, KY 40503

Dear Dr. Hager,

In 2002 President George W. Bush picked you—a prominent OB/GYN—to advise the Food and Drug Administration on women's reproductive health medications. This should have been a joyous occasion, but sadly you were also in the midst of a divorce. As a faithful Christian, I expect that was especially painful.

Also painful? Getting anally raped for years and years.

You see, Dr. Hager, your wife, Linda, alleged that you forcibly sodomized her on many occasions during your 30-year marriage. According to her, when she once confronted you, you feigned ignorance, claiming that you couldn't "feel the difference" between her God-anointed lady business and her bad place.

This sort of sexual deviance would seem to contradict the spirit of your book *As Jesus Cared for Women*, in which you lay out the case against birth control (it promotes promiscuity, and you refuse to prescribe it for unmarried women) and suggest reading scripture to alleviate the symptoms of PMS.

So . . . there's your adviser on women's reproductive drugs: A gynecologist who prescribes 50 mg of Jesus for cramps, hates birth control, and (if we're to take Linda at her word) can't tell the difference between an anus and a vagina.

Sorry, Dr. Hager, but whether true or not, Linda's allegations will forever taint your reputation, and you'll always be the butt of stinging cracks. I only pray you're not fingered by Bush for any more appointments. The women of this country deserve better.

Gently,

U.S. DEPARTMENT OF HOMELAND APOLOGY

DR. W. DAVID HAGER
1720 NICHOLASVILLE RD., 5TH FLOOR, BLDG. E
LEXINGTON, KY 40503

SOUTHERNERS
c/o The Alamo
300 Alamo Plaza
San Antonio, TX 78205

Dear Southerners,

Prejudice is alive and well in the United States. Take the fact that millions of Americans automatically dismiss anyone with a southern accent as "stupid" or "ignorant."

Gone are the days when the accent evoked images of bow-tied gentlemen sipping mint juleps on a shady front porch, "yes ma'am/no sir" manners, and down-home cookin'. These have been replaced with images of NASCAR-sponsored BBQ sauce, megachurches with secretly gay pastors, and super-sized people shopping for XXL "Git R Done" T-shirts at Wal-Mart.

So why the paradigm shift? Why has the southerner stereotype gone from genteel to dumb? After careful analysis, I've traced it back to a hot July day in 1953, when a young George W. Bush decided to become the only member of his family to adopt a southern accent. As president, Mr. Bush became the de facto spokesman for all southerners, a role he seemed to relish. That oversized-belt-buckle swagger. That nod to the southern pronunciation of his middle initial. That "aw shucks" persona. That rugged rancher ethos.

Heck, it was almost enough to make you forget that he was a Yankee-born, Yale- and Harvard-bred multimillionaire who didn't own a ranch until he was fifty-three years old.

So let me apologize on behalf of the northerners, urbanites, and snobbish intellectuals who equate your drawl with dimwittedness. "Dubya" doesn't speak for all y'all, and having an accent doesn't make somebody stupid.

Being stupid makes somebody stupid.

Ride along now,

U.S. DEPARTMENT OF HOMELAND APOLOGY

SOUTHERNERS
C/O THE ALAMO
300 ALAMO PLAZA
SAN ANTONIO, TX 78205

THE ECONOMY

c/o Board of Governors of the Federal Reserve System
20th St. and Constitution Ave. NW
Washington, DC 20551

Dear Economy,

I'm sorry, old friend. You're a tough SOB, and you can take a helluva beating, but over these past eight years, George Bush has whooped you like a drunken stepdaddy.

He slashed taxes even as he requested hundreds of billions in war funding and other new spending. To finance those tax cuts, we've had to raid the Social Security and Medicare funds, further weakening institutions that are projected to go bust in our lifetimes.

When Bush took office, we had a budget surplus of $230 billion. By his second term, he had turned that into a $248 billion deficit. On his watch, our national debt has ballooned to more than $9 trillion, and it keeps growing at $1.4+ billion a day. That's $1 million a minute. We've run up such a tab on our federal credit card that we'd have to spend more than $20 billion a month just to keep up with the interest—more than the cost of fighting in Iraq and Afghanistan combined.

And the average family's slice of the $1.6 trillion spent on those wars through 2017: $46,400. That's about the cost of sending a student to the University of Alabama, with room and board, for four years.

Americans have taken a cue from Bush's spending habits. By 2007 we'd accumulated almost $1 trillion in credit card debt. By the time Bush leaves his Washington home, hundreds of thousands of Americans will have left theirs, unable to keep up with mortgage payments.

Add soaring energy prices, slumping consumer confidence, and tanking dollar to the mix, and you've got the Bush Diet, "guaranteed to dramatically shrink the waistline of any economy in just eight short years or your money back."*

Fiducially,

*Just kidding about the money-back part. It's all gone.

U.S. DEPARTMENT OF HOMELAND APOLOGY
2009 · 2001
MISTAKES · WERE MADE

THE ECONOMY
C/O BOARD OF GOVERNORS OF THE FEDERAL RESERVE SYSTEM
20TH ST. AND CONSTITUTION AVE. NW
WASHINGTON, DC 20551

YALE UNIVERSITY
Office of Public Affairs
265 Church St., Suite 901
New Haven, CT 06511

Dear Yale,

With a proud academic tradition dating back four centuries, you have long been considered one of the world's finest institutions of higher learning.

Your stunning campus is home to America's third-largest library system, with some 12.5 million volumes. You have an 8.9 percent acceptance rate, and boast an endowment of $22.5 billion, allowing you to give considerable scholarships to many of the brightest young minds in the world. Your alumni include 19 Nobel laureates, 18 Supreme Court justices, 523 members of Congress, and countless luminaries from the worlds of business, science, and the arts.

You're also the school that looked at George W. Bush's application and said, "Yee-haw!"

Yes, his father and grandfather were alums. Yes, he came from a wealthy family (which, let's face it, never hurts when applying to an Ivy League school). But legacies have their limits, Yale. Financial gain has to be weighed against academic credibility—namely, the credibility one stands to lose by admitting a special-needs student.

I'm sorry, Yale. If it's any consolation, those bastards at Harvard actually gave the guy an MBA.

Warm regards,

YALE UNIVERSITY
OFFICE OF PUBLIC AFFAIRS
265 CHURCH ST., SUITE 901
NEW HAVEN, CT 06511

CUSTODIAL STAFF
Louisiana Superdome
Sugar Bowl Dr.
New Orleans, LA 70112

Dear Custodial Staff,

In the first days after Hurricane Katrina, the Superdome was turned into a makeshift refugee camp. Thousands of people who'd lost everything (including loved ones) huddled there for days, desperately waiting for food, water . . . *anything* to arrive from the U.S. government.

But nothing came. In fact, on the morning Katrina made landfall, George W. Bush—the head of our government—was standing on a runway in Arizona, presenting John McCain with a birthday cake. The next day, he played guitar with country singer Mark Wills before heading back to his ranch in Crawford for a good night's rest.

Meanwhile, the Superdome's ventilation system failed, making the heat unbearable. The toilets backed up, covering the floor with excrement and creating a nauseating stench. Stranded and desperate, people took to using trashcans as toilets. Garbage piles reached twenty feet in one of the parking garages. There were reports of violent attacks, of rapes. One man jumped to his death. Others simply died.

It wasn't until day three that the president finally saw the Superdome with his own eyes (as he flew over New Orleans on his way back to Washington).

He probably couldn't tell from Air Force One, but the once-proud home to political conventions and championship games had become a concentrated cesspool of sweat, feces, urine, blood, trash, and corpses.

Sorry you had to clean that up.

All the best,

U.S. DEPARTMENT OF HOMELAND APOLOGY
MISTAKES WERE MADE
2001 2009

CUSTODIAL STAFF
LOUISIANA SUPERDOME
SUGAR BOWL DR.
NEW ORLEANS, LA 70112

MS. ANN COULTER

c/o Clare Boothe Luce Policy Institute
112 Elden St., Suite P
Herdon, VA 20170

Dear Ann,

You gorgeous bitch.

Of all the people who deserve an apology for eight years of Bush, you just about take the cake. I've seen you subjected to a barrage of body blows since the 2000 election. Demonized. Crucified. Labeled a "hatemonger" and a Nazi. Wished dead who knows how many times. Some idiots have even stooped to mocking your appearance.

You didn't deserve it, and I'm sorry you had to endure it.

Truth is, those liberals who get all riled up at the mere mention of your name are missing the point (not to mention playing right into your famously elongated hands).

You're no bigot, Ann. Hell, you're no Nazi, either. You're just another white girl from Connecticut who wasn't about to be another white girl from Connecticut. You were smart enough to read the tea leaves back in the 1990s. Smart enough to realize that extremism would be the new black.

I may disagree with most of your "opinions." I may even feel like vomiting when I see you desperately trying to slither into the news cycle by calling John Edwards a "faggot." But the truth is . . . I need you on that wall.

I need you out there spewing that beautiful crazy. That crazy lets me know there's still a world that scares the shit out of the people who scare the shit out of me. That crazy is my hot cocoa on a winter's night. And there's nobody I'd rather share it with, gorgeous. Nobody at all.

All my love,

U.S. DEPARTMENT OF HOMELAND APOLOGY
2001 • MISTAKES • 2009
HERE AGAIN

AFFIX
POSTAGE
HERE

MS. ANN COULTER
C/O CLARE BOOTHE LUCE POLICY INSTITUTE
112 ELDEN ST., SUITE P
HERDON, VA 20170

VICE PRESIDENT RICHARD CHENEY

The White House
1600 Pennsylvania Ave. NW
Washington, DC 20500

Dear Mr. Vice President,

By the close of the twentieth century, you seemed to have it all.

You'd been White House chief of staff, a five-term congressman, and secretary of defense. You'd made a fortune in the private sector. You had a lovely family. You were learning to control your ever-present sneer. You were rich, accomplished, and respected.

And then you threw it all away.

In 2000 George W. Bush asked you to become his running mate. You said yes. What followed were eight of the worst years of your life:

- Your chief of staff was sentenced to prison.
- Your daughter became the focus of your boss's stupid gay-marriage crusade.
- You had multiple health scares and a defibrillator implanted to keep you alive.
- You were the chief architect of a disastrous war waged on false pretenses.
- You were accused of abusing power and illegally withholding documents.
- You were accused of letting oil companies dictate energy policy.
- You shot your friend in the face.

Instead of being remembered as one of the great public servants of the twentieth century, you'll be remembered as one of the Nixonian villains of the twenty-first.

Mr. Vice President, I think I speak for your loved ones, future generations of historians, and all Americans when I say, "I'm sorry you ever met George W. Bush."

Regrettably,

AFFIX
POSTAGE
HERE

VICE PRESIDENT RICHARD CHENEY
THE WHITE HOUSE
1600 PENNSYLVANIA AVE. NW
WASHINGTON, DC 20500

PRESIDENT GEORGE W. BUSH
The White House
1600 Pennsylvania Ave. NW
Washington, DC 20500

Dear Mr. President,

You've been demonized and belittled more than any president in recent history—perhaps all of history. You've been labeled dimwitted, evil.

I don't think you're "evil," Mr. President. Hell, I don't think you're stupid, either.

What I think is that you're painfully insecure.

You like to give people nicknames. Any first-year psych student will tell you that is a form of bullying, a way of bringing people down a notch. There's your ten-gallon swagger, overcompensation for a crippling lack of self-esteem. And there's your habit of nervously smiling after a declarative sentence, desperately hoping it meets with approval.

Mr. President, I believe this insecurity can even explain some of your (seemingly endless) policy failures. For instance, your rampant cronyism and huge tax breaks for the rich stem from a deep need to be liked by those around you (as does your constant pandering to the religious right). Your refusal to listen to dissenting opinions is a function of your fragile ego; even constructive disagreements are too much to bear.

But it's your biggest blunder that really speaks to the heart of this insecurity: your decision to invade Iraq. I believe that decision was, at the very least, hastened by your need to win the respect of your father. After all those years being the wandering, occasionally drunken son of an important man—here was your chance to make it right. As a precursor to war, you even called Saddam the "guy who tried to kill my dad."

I'm sorry, Mr. President, but it seems that for all your wealth and power, you're just another son trying to win his daddy's love. And for all your Texan machismo, you're really just one chromosome away from being a stripper.

Sincerely,

U.S. DEPARTMENT OF HOMELAND APOLOGY

PRESIDENT GEORGE W. BUSH
THE WHITE HOUSE
1600 PENNSYLVANIA AVE. NW
WASHINGTON, DC 20500

THE FUTURE
c/o Institute for the Future
124 University Ave., 2nd Floor
Palo Alto, California 94301

Dear Future,

I'm sorry we used up all the oil.

I'm sorry Osama Bin Laden lived to be 116.

I'm sorry Topeka, Kansas, is a beach community.

I'm sorry the former United States of America is now the Christian Republic of Republican Christians (CRRC) and the Godless Emirate of Homosexual Abortion Lovers (GEHAL).

I'm sorry Bill O'Reilly went crazy and killed all those children.

I'm sorry Social Security went bankrupt.

I'm sorry about all the wars over fresh water.

I'm sorry extremism is still flourishing in the Middle East.

I'm sorry we failed to recognize the dangers of unchecked population growth.

I'm sorry the Supreme Court elected George W. Bush in 2000.

I'm sorry we elected him in 2004.

I'm sorry we left the place such a mess.

Faithfully,

U.S. DEPARTMENT OF HOMELAND APOLOGY

2001 · 2009

MISTAKES WERE MADE

THE FUTURE
C/O INSTITUTE FOR THE FUTURE
124 UNIVERSITY AVE., 2ND FLOOR
PALO ALTO, CALIFORNIA 94301

SEN. BARACK OBAMA
713 Hart Senate Office Building
Washington, D.C. 20510

Dear Senator Obama,

On January 31, 2007, George W. Bush had this to say of you: "He's articulate."

Some people took that as a subtle dig at your African heritage. As if the president was surprised that a black man—albeit one with some of Mr. Bush's own glorious white blood flowing in his veins—could have such a command of the English language.

But I think that misses the point. Having George W. Bush praise your speaking skills is a net negative no matter what your ethnicity happens to be.

It's like Stevie Wonder praising your painting skills, or Jessica Simpson calling you "intelligent." Considering the source, the compliment is, frankly, insulting.

Senator Obama, I believe President Bush owes you an apology for giving you a compliment.

Articulately,

U.S. DEPARTMENT OF HOMELAND APOLOGY
"MISTAKES WERE MADE" 2001 2009

SEN. BARACK OBAMA
713 HART SENATE OFFICE BUILDING
WASHINGTON, D.C. 20510

SEN. JOHN MCCAIN
241 Russell Senate Office Bldg.
Washington, DC 20510

Dear Senator McCain,

You're a smart man, Senator. An honorable man. Only the dimwitted or blindly partisan would question that. But for the life of me, sir, I'll never understand why you decided to hitch your political wagon to George W. Bush.

Forget his abysmal poll numbers. Forget his penchant for scandal, his theocratic ideology, and his deficits (which make your beloved Ronald Reagan do cartwheels in his grave).

If the rumors are true, Senator, then Mr. Bush tried to destroy you during the 2000 primaries with the rumor that you'd fathered an illegitimate black child (in fact, you have a dark-skinned daughter, Bridget, whom you adopted from Mother Teresa's orphanage in Bangladesh). If the rumors are true, Senator, this guy went after your family.

And what did you do? You, the tough-as-nails fighter pilot who spent five years getting tortured in Vietnam. The "straight-talker" who promised to hunt down Osama Bin Laden even if it meant following him to the "gates of hell."

You hugged him, helped him get reelected, and supported his disastrous war.

Senator, you'll forgive me for being so early twenty-first century, but—wtf?

Whether America agreed with your positions or not, at least we agreed that you were a man of principle. But watching you suckle Bush's teat over these past eight years has been, well . . .

. . . torture.

Shine on,

U.S. DEPARTMENT OF HOMELAND APOLOGY

SEN. JOHN McCAIN
241 RUSSELL SENATE OFFICE BLDG.
WASHINGTON, DC 20510

THE FORTY-FOURTH PRESIDENT OF THE UNITED STATES

The White House
1600 Pennsylvania Ave. NW
Washington, DC 20500

Dear Sir or Madam,

Welcome to the White House. A little hard to get your head around, isn't it? You're the President of the United States! Schools will be named after you. Arguments over you will ruin countless family dinners. You have your own chef, your own jumbo jet, your own nuclear arsenal.

You also have a lot of work to do.

A slumping economy. A ravaged environment. Hatred for America around the world. A dangerous national debt. Millions of Americans without healthcare. A growing energy crisis. An overburdened military. Vanishing American jobs. Antiquated educational standards. Iraq. Afghanistan. Iran. North Korea. China. Russia. Venezuela. A deeply divided America.

Nobody expects you to fix all of them. Or even half of them, for that matter. But they expect you to try.

These next four to eight years will be the busiest and richest of your life. On your journey, I ask that you keep two of your predecessors in mind:

James Buchanan is regarded as one of America's worst presidents. On his watch, the country became deeply divided, increasingly corrupt, and totally ineffectual. States began to break away from the Union, and America seemed doomed to failure. And then his successor arrived. Through boldness and genius, Abraham Lincoln became the savior of the Union and perhaps our greatest president. No pressure.

As the saying goes, it's always darkest before dawn. Perhaps that makes you the dawn. Or perhaps you'll be merely an extension of the darkness. I guess that's up to you. We've handed you the keys. Our country and our futures are in your hands.

Don't screw it up.

Sincerely,

WE'RE MAKE MISTAKES

POSTAGE
HERE

THE FORTY-FOURTH PRESIDENT OF THE UNITED STATES
THE WHITE HOUSE
1600 PENNSYLVANIA AVE. NW
WASHINGTON, DC 20500

★★★ SOURCES ★★★

Abstinent Teens
"Abstinence Programs Not Effective, Study Finds"
  (*Associated Press* 4/13/07)
"How Effective Are Abstinence Pledges?"
  (*BBC News* 6/29/04)
"Reborn a Virgin: Adolescents' Retracting of Virginity
  Pledges and Sexual Histories"
  (*American Journal of Public Health* [vol. 96, no. 6] 6/06)
"Study: Abstinence Classes Don't Stop Sex"
  (*USA Today* 4/14/07)

African Americans
"Bush Criticizes NAACP's Leadership"
  (*Washington Post* 7/10/04)
"Bush Says He's 'Unfamiliar' with Voting Rights Act"
  (*Sacramento Observer* 2/9/05)
"A Polling Free-Fall Among Blacks"
  (*Washington Post* 10/13/05)

American Children
"Late Twist for Health Insurance Coverage"
  (*Associated Press* 12/25/07)
"Who Are America's Poor Children?"
  (*National Center for Children in Poverty* 12/06)
"Poverty Rate Up 3rd Year in a Row"
  (*Washington Post* 8/27/04)

Big Oil
"Chevron Redubs Ship Named for Bush Aide"
  (*San Francisco Chronicle* 3/5/01)
"Oil Executives Lobbied on Drilling"
  (*Washington Post* 2/27/02)
"U.S. Retail Gas Prices" (eia.doe.gov)
"Exxon Mobil Amasses Record $36B 2005 Profit"
  (*USA Today* 1/30/06)
"World's Ten Biggest Corporations"
  (*Fortune Global 500* 2007)
"Over a Barrel" (*The Guardian* 1/8/08)

Osama Bin Laden
"Lost at Tora Bora" (*New York Times Magazine* 9/11/05)
Berntsen, Gary, and Ralph Pezzullo, *Jawbreaker: The Attack
  on Bin Laden and Al Qaeda: A Personal Account by the
  CIA's Key Field Commander* (Crown, 2005)

President James Buchanan
Stampp, Kenneth M., *America in 1857: A Nation on the
  Brink* (Oxford University Press, 1990)

The Buck
"President Addresses the Nation in Prime Time Press
  Conference" (White House transcript 4/13/04)

President George H. W. Bush
"Bush Faces New Round of Drug Questions"
  (*CNN* 8/20/99)

"Bush Angrily Denounces Report of Extramarital Affair as
  'a Lie'" (*Washington Post* 8/12/92)
"Bush Acknowledges 1976 DUI Charge" (*CNN* 11/2/00)
Woodward, Bob, *Plan of Attack* (Simon & Schuster, 2004)

President George W. Bush
"Bush Calls Saddam 'The Guy Who Tried to Kill My
  Dad'" (*CNN* 9/27/02)
"How Many More Mike Browns Are Out There?"
  (*Time* 9/25/05)

Dr. Richard Carmona
"Surgeon General Sees 4-Year Term as Compromised"
  (*New York Times* 7/11/07)
"Ex–Surgeon General Says White House Hushed Him"
  (*Washington Post* 7/11/07)

President Fidel Castro
"Bush Took Quote Out of Context, Researcher Says"
  (*Los Angeles Times* 7/20/04)

Vice President Richard Cheney
"18%?" (Washington Post 3/5/06)
"The Cheney Branch of Government" (*Time* 6/22/07)
"Clay Co-Sponsors Resolution to Impeach Cheney"
  (*Associated Press* 5/2/07)
"Sources: Cheney Curses Senator Over Halliburton
  Criticism" (*CNN* 6/25/04)

Mr. Richard Clarke
"'01 Memo to Rice Warned of Qaeda and Offered Plan"
  (*New York Times* 2/12/05)
Clarke, Richard A., *Against All Enemies: Inside America's
  War on Terror* (Simon & Schuster, 2004)

Sen. Max Cleland
"Dirty-Bomb Politics" (*Washington Post* 6/20/02)
"Cleland Defeated by Conservative" (*USA Today* 11/6/02)

Mr. Adam Clymer
"Bush: No Apology for Gaffe" (*BBC News* 9/5/00)
"Carey McWilliams Award Winners" (apsanet.org)
"Drunken Driving Lawsuit Settled"
  (*New York Times* 5/22/92)

Conservatives
"The Debt to the Penny and Who Holds It"
  (treasurydirect.gov)
"Buckley: Bush Not a True Conservative"
  (*CBS News* 7/22/06)

Ms. Ann Coulter
"9/11 Commissioner Criticizes Coulter's 'Hate-Filled
  Attack'" (*USA Today* 6/9/06)
"Coulter Under Fire for Anti-Gay Slur" (*CNN* 3/4/07)

★★★ SOURCES ★★★

Sen. Larry Craig
"More Gay Men Describe Sexual Encounters with U.S.
  Sen. Craig" (*Idaho Statesman* 12/3/07)
"Senator Larry Craig: 'I Am Not Gay'" (*Fox News* 8/28/07)
"Pressure Mounts on Larry Craig to Resign"
  (*Fox News* 8/31/07)
"Not Being True to Himself" (*Time* 10/8/06)
"Haggard Admits 'Sexual Immorality,' Apologizes"
  (*MSNBC* 11/5/06)

The Residents of Crawford, Texas
"Bush Vacation Puts Spotlight on Tiny Crawford"
  (*CNN* 8/7/01)
"Washington's August Break: Just Don't Call It Vacation
  Time" (*Bloomberg* 8/8/07)
"Memorial to Troops Killed in Iraq Is Vandalized in Texas"
  (*New York Times* 8/16/05)
"Souvenirs Become Hard Sell in Crawford"
  (*Philadelphia Inquirer* 2/8/07)

The People of Darfur
"UN: 6-Month Setback for Darfur Peacekeeping Because
  of Inadequate Troops, Equipment and Security"
  (*International Herald Tribune* 1/9/08)
"2 Charged in Darfur War Crimes"
  (*San Francisco Chronicle* 2/28/07)
"Death and Deception in Darfur"
  (*Washington Post* 7/31/04)

The Dixie Chicks
"DJs Suspended for Playing Dixie Chicks"
  (*USA Today* 5/8/03)
"Dixie Chicks Pulled from Air after Bashing Bush"
  (*CNN* 3/14/03)
"Courtesy of the Red, White & Blue"
  (*60 Minutes II* 10/29/03)
"Taking the Dixie Out of the Chicks"
  (*Miami Herald* 6/4/06)

The Economy
"The Economic Consequences of Mr. Bush"
  (*Vanity Fair* 11/24/07)
"National Debt Grows $1 Million a Minute"
  (*Associated Press* 12/3/07)
"Consumer Bankruptcy Filings Rose 40% in '07"
  (*Wall Street Journal* 1/4/08)
"Economic Costs of Iraq, Afghanistan Wars Put at $1.6
  Trillion So Far, About $20,900 Per Family"
  (Associated Press 11/14/07)
"Credit Card Debt Spikes to Six-Month High"
  (*CNN* Money 1/8/08)
"Cost of Attendance" (cost.ua.edu)

Her Majesty Queen Elizabeth II
"Queen Triumphs Amid Bush Gaffes" (*BBC News* 5/9/07)

Mr. Siegfried Engelmann and Ms. Elaine C. Bruner
"In Video Message, Bin Laden Issues Warning to U.S."
  (*New York Times* 10/30/04)
Eengelmann, Sigfried, and Elaine C. Bruner, *Reading
  Mastery—Level 2 Storybook 1* (Reading Mastery:
  Rainbow Edition) (McGraw-Hill, 1997)

The Environment
"Bush's Policies in Texas Prompt Heated Exchanges in
  Debate" (*New York Times* 10/12/00)
"In Search of a Moment for the Ages in Six Hours of
  High-Stakes Debate" (*Associated Press* 10/14/04)
"The Bush Record" (nrdc.org)
"Bush Vetoes Water Bill" (*St. Petersburg Times* 11/3/07)

Family Values
"The Profitable Business of War" (*Salon* 9/27/04)
"Bush Angrily Denounces Report of Extramarital Affair as
  'a Lie'" (*Washington Post* 8/12/92)
"The Relatively Charmed Life of Neil Bush"
  (*Washington Post* 12/28/03)
"Mrs. Bush Should Shop for a Moral Compass"
  (*Chicago Sun-Times* 6/27/99)
"Noelle Bush Heads Back to Rehab" (*USA Today* 7/19/02)
Metro-Dade Police Department Report
  (December 31, 1994)
"Florida Gov. Jeb Bush's Son Arrested"
  (*Associated Press* 9/17/05)
"Bush Acknowledges 1976 DUI Charge" (*CNN* 11/2/00)

People of France
"House Now Serving 'Freedom Fries'" (*Fox News* 3/11/03)
"Ex-Rep. Bob Ney Gets 30 Months in Jail"
  (*CBS News* 1/19/07)

Gay Republicans
"'Homosexuality Isn't Natural or Healthy'"
  (*ABC News* 6/7/07)
"Senator Larry Craig: 'I Am Not Gay'"
  (*Fox News* 8/28/07)
"Not Being True to Himself" (*Time* 10/8/06)

Mr. Alberto Gonzales
"Maybe Gonzales Won't Recall His Painful Day on the
  Hill" (*Washington Post* 4/20/07)
"New Gene Linked to Alzheimer's"
  (*Washington Post* 1/15/07)

Vice President Al Gore
"Bush Targets Venezuela's Chavez in Tough Speech"
  (*New York Times* 11/6/05)

Dr. David Hager
"Dr. Hager's Family Values" (*The Nation* 5/30/05)
Hager, W. David, M.D., As Jesus Cared for Women:
  Restoring Women Then and Now
  (Fleming H. Revell, 1998)

Mr. William K. Hampton
Second Judicial Court Arrest/Notice to Appear/Probable
  Cause Affidavit (thesmokinggun.com 1/20/01)

People of Iran
"The Myth of the All-Powerful Ahmadinejad"
  (*Asia Times* 10/5/07)
"Iraq Weapons—Made in Iran?" (*ABC News* 3/6/06)

Mr. Dean Kamen
"Bush Fails the Segway Test" (*BBC News* 6/14/03)
"The Science of Segway" (segway.com)

L'Oréal
"Harris's Election Stance Assailed; Head of Rights Panel
    Probing Fla. Vote Calls Her Answers 'Laughable'"
    (*Washington Post* 1/13/01)

Mr. Rush Limbaugh
"Medicare Drug Benefit May Cost $1.2 Trillion"
    (*Washington Post* 2/9/05)
"Medicare Debate Turns to Pricing of Drug Benefits"
    (*New York Times* 11/24/03)
"GOP Revolt over What Defines Us"
    (*San Diego Union Tribune* 9/21/06)
"Limbaugh Admits Addiction to Pain Medication"
    (*CNN* 10/10/03)

Sen. John McCain
"The Anatomy of a Smear Campaign"
    (*Boston Globe* 3/21/04)
"The Bush-McCain Love-Hate Relationship"
    (*MSNBC* 3/12/04)
"Wooing New Hampshire's Undeclared"
    (*Time* 1/7/08)

Mr. Scott McClellan
"Press Briefing by Scott McClellan—10/10/03"
    (whitehouse.gov)
"Former Aide Blames Bush for Leak Deceit"
    (*ABC News* 11/21/07)
"Jeff Gannon Admits Past 'Mistakes,' Berates Critics"
    (*Washington Post* 2/19/05)
"Rove-Gannon Connection?" (*CBS News* 2/18/05)

Her Excellency Angela Merkel
"Bush's Backrub of Merkel Tickles Web's Funny Bone"
    (*Associated Press* 7/21/06)

The Middle Class
"American Workers Get Short Shrift"
    (*Augusta Chronicle* 9/16/06)
"Everything's Up" (*Columbus Dispatch* 5/22/06)
"U.S. Retail Gas Prices" (eia.doe.gov)
"Bush: Protectionism Will Cost U.S. Jobs"
    (*Associated Press* 10/14/07)
"Bush Urged to Extend Capital Gains, Dividend Tax
    Cuts" (Bloomberg 1/10/08)
"Drop Foreseen in Median Price of U.S. Homes"
    (*New York Times* 8/26/07)

Ms. Harriet Miers
"Documents Show Supreme Court Nominee's Close Ties
    to Bush" (*New York Times* 10/11/05)
"Nomination Was Plagued by Missteps from the Start"
    (*Washington Post* 10/28/05)
"In Speeches, Miers Heaped Praise on President"
    (*Los Angeles Times* 10/18/05)
"House Democrats Pass Contempt Citations"
    (*The Guardian* 7/25/07)
"Justice Dept. Sets Criminal Inquiry on C.I.A. Tapes"
    (*New York Times* 1/3/08)

Mr. Michael Moore
"'Chicago' Triumphs at Oscars" (*CNN* 3/24/03)
"Bush Clings To Dubious Allegations About Iraq"
    (*Washington Post* 3/18/03)

Mr. Paul O'Neill
Suskind, Ron, *The Price of Loyalty: George W. Bush, the
    White House, and the Education of Paul O'Neill*
    (Simon & Schuster, 2004)
"Administration Reports Benefit Shortfall Totals $45 Trillion
    over Next 75 Years" (*Associated Press* 12/17/07)
"Greenspan Is Critical of Bush in Memoir"
    (*Washington Post* 9/15/07)

Mr. Bill O'Reilly
"Bill O'Reilly's Bullying Ways Merit Apology"
    (*Denver Post* 10/25/05)
"Fox Host Rips Perdue on Dance for Whites"
    (*Atlanta Journal Constitution* 5/7/03)
"Talk Host's Towering Rant: S.F. Not Worth Saving"
    (*San Francisco Chronicle* 11/11/05)
"Bad Rap Forces Pepsi to Drop Ludacris
    (*The Guardian* 8/30/02)
O'Reilly, Bill, *Those Who Trespass: A Novel of Television
    and Murder* (Broadway Books, 2004)

Ms. Valerie Plame-Wilson
"Armitage Admits Leaking Plame's Identity" (*CNN* 9/8/06)
"What Valerie Plame Really Did at the CIA"
    (*The Nation* 9/6/06)
"Leak of Agent's Name Causes Exposure of CIA Front
    Firm" (*Washington Post* 10/4/03)
"The Spy Next Door" (*Washington Post* 10/8/03)

General Colin Powell (Ret.)
Powell, Colin L., *My American Journey: An Autobiography.*
    (Random House, 1995)
"U.S. Secretary of State Colin Powell Addresses the U.N.
    Security Council" (whitehouse.gov)
"Powell Calls Pre-Iraq U.N. Speech a 'Blot' on his Record"
    (*USA Today* 9/8/05)

Pretzels
"Bush on Fainting Episode: 'Chew Your Food'"
    (*CNN* 1/14/02)

Vice President Dan Quayle
"Dan Quayle Leaves John Mellencamp Concert After Bush
    Comment" (*Associated Press* 7/21/06)

Science
"Bush Endorses 'Intelligent Design'" (*Boston Globe* 8/2/05)
"Bush Calls for Action to Reduce Greenhouse Gases"
    (*International Herald-Tribune* 5/31/07)
"Warnings on Drilling Reversed" (*Washington Post* 4/7/02)
"Abortion Foe to Be Reappointed to FDA Panel"
    (*Washington Post* 6/29/04}
"Nobel Laureates Back Stem Cell Research"
    (*Washington Post* 2/22/01)

Gen. Eric Shinseki (Ret.)
"New Strategy Vindicates Ex–Army Chief Shinseki"
    (*New York Times* 1/12/07)
"Scorned General's Tactics Proved Right"
    (*The Guardian* 3/29/03)

★★★ SOURCES ★★★

The Superdome Custodial Staff
"Video Footage Shows Bush, Chertoff Were Warned of
Katrina's Potential Impact" (*Associated Press* 3/2/06)
"Out of the Nightmare, into the Astrodome"
(*Salon* 9/2/05)
"Katrina Timeline" (thinkprogress.org)

Target
"Ex-Aide to Bush Pleads Guilty" (*Washington Post* 8/5/06)
"Former White House Adviser Pleads Guilty to Theft"
(*Associated Press* 8/4/06)

Teachers
"Teachers Paid an Average Salary of $46,752, Survey
Finds" (*USA Today* 6/25/05)
"House GOP Sustains Bush Veto of Health Bill"
(*Associated Press* 11/16/07)
"Bush Deflects Criticism on 'No Child Left Behind'"
(*CNN* 1/3/04)
"Paige Calls NEA 'Terrorist Organization'"
(*CNN* 2/23/04)

The United States Armed Forces
"Military Spouses Outraged by Extended Deployments"
(*Chicago Tribune* 4/12/07)
"Body Armor Saves Lives in Iraq; Pentagon Criticized for
Undersupply of Protective Vests"
(*Washington Post* 12/4/03)
"Junk Becomes Troops' Treasure"
(*Milwaukee Journal Sentinel* 6/12/05)
"Troops Could Lose Raise in Combat Pay"
(*Seattle Post-Intelligencer* 8/15/03)
"Mold, Leaky Roofs Beset VA Clinics"
(*Associated Press* 3/21/07)

Mr. Harry M. Whittington
"Cheney Shoots Fellow Hunter in Mishap on a Texas
Ranch" (*New York Times* 2/23/06)

Women
"Women's Group Urges Bush Panel to Hold the Line on
Title IX" (*Associated Press* 1/28/03)
"Bush May End Offices Dealing with Women's Issues,
Groups Say" (*New York Times* 12/19/01)
"U.S. Policy Blamed for Abortion Deaths in Ethiopia"
(*San Francisco Chronicle* 12/12/03)

Yale University
"Yale Facts" (yale.edu)
"About Yale/History" (yale.edu)